What people are saying about …

STRONGER

"I know Jim Daly. He's a man of courage and strength. There's not a better person who could write a book entitled *Stronger*. Jim shares with readers in a wonderful way that, yes, there are times when you are kicked squarely in the teeth by life. But he leads us in the direction of the *real* source of strength. If you've found hurts, disappointments, and trials in your world you'll be uplifted by the insight and wisdom of Jim Daly in this wonderful book, *Stronger*."

Kevin Leman, New York Times best-selling
author of *Have a New Kid by Friday, Have a New
Husband by Friday,* and *Have a New You by Friday*

"What a wonderful change of perspective! If you have ever wondered how on earth to apply the biblical exhortation to rejoice in your trials or be content in all things, you have got to read this book. You will never look at life in quite the same way again."

Shaunti Feldhahn, best-selling
author of *For Women Only*

"In the midst of difficult life situations, we are often tempted to ask the question: Why, God? This book gives an answer. In these pages, Jim Daly reminds us that pain is an opportunity to grow. Whatever your pain, whatever your struggle, this book offers an abundance of insight into how you can use the pain and struggles in your life to lean more toward God and His healing and loving power."

Richard Stearns, president of World Vision, U.S., and author of *The Hole in Our Gospel*

"Jesus never promised His followers a perpetual Disney experience here on earth. I know firsthand that God is with us even when darkness is all around us. Jim Daly does a great job of describing what it's like to walk through the valley of the shadow of death and what life is like on the other side."

Brady Boyd, senior pastor of New Life Church

"Life has its challenges. When I learned I had late-stage cancer, I had to decide whether I would be a victim or a victor. Although I survived my crisis, it would have been easier if I had this book available to me. Jim Daly teaches us how to take crises and attack them with the Word of God. This inspirational work helps us learn how to respond when we are 'down and out.' Whenever life seems to be treating you unfairly, grab *Stronger* and pray through the principles offered in its pages. Like me, you can be more than a survivor—you can be stronger!"

Bishop Harry R. Jackson Jr., senior pastor of Hope Christian Church and founder and president of High Impact Leadership Coalition

"The Christian life is sometimes made out to be a bed of roses, but we do endure many hardships, like anyone in this fallen world. Jim

Daly definitely makes that clear through countless stories of people who have gone through heartwrenching and painful experiences—but the key is that they found their hope in God and that the Lord used those times to bring them closer to Himself. The point that Jim makes in this book is something Jesus talks about in John 16:33: 'In the world you will have tribulation; but be of good cheer, I have overcome the world.'"

Ron Luce, president and founder
of Teen Mania Ministries

"I have known Jim Daly for twenty years, and I know of no one better to write about the strength of character God can bring from life's challenges. Throughout his early life, Jim had more than his share of adversity. Yet, as he says in the book, he didn't just *survive.* Through God's strength, he got *stronger.* Readers will be encouraged by story after story of others who found similar strength through their relationship with God. I commend this book to anyone desiring to experience greater victory through, not in spite of, life's hardships."

David "Mac" McQuiston, president
and CEO of CEO Forum, Inc.

"Jim Daly's book *Stronger* is an excellent treatise on real faith. It is not a 'high church' document but a real-life, gut-level treatment of life as it really is and happens to each of us. Jim uses his personal life and stories to color the picture of challenges each of us faces on a regular basis. He doesn't stop there but offers scriptural remedies and comfort and support for the journey. *Stronger* is Jim's story, but, in fact, it's everyone's story. I highly recommend this beautiful book of help, love, and compassion."

Steve Largent, president and CEO of CTIA
and former NFL player and U.S. Congressman

"The pages of this book are filled with encouragement and hope that are only found when an author has personally experienced the deep love of God. No matter how disappointed you may be with life, this is a reminder of how powerful our Savior is. His power overcomes every circumstance and is available to any one of us. Thanks for speaking directly to me, Jim. I needed a good dose of hope, and now my hope is renewed."

Tom Davis, CEO of Children's HopeChest and
author of *Red Letters* and *Fields of the Fatherless*

"Jim tackles one of the most sensitive and difficult areas in the Christian life. What is God doing when pain, tragedy, depression, and suffering come into our lives? Through stories of many transformed lives, including his own, Jim draws us to useful and powerful scriptural principles. These principles can, if we're ready to submit and be broken and renewed, make us stronger in faith and character and mighty in His strength for the kingdom."

Pat Gelsinger, president and COO of EMC
Corporation and author of *The Juggling Act*

STRONGER

STRONGER

Trading Brokenness for **Unbreakable Strength**

JIM DALY

WITH JAMES LUND

David C Cook

transforming lives together

STRONGER
Published by David C. Cook
4050 Lee Vance View
Colorado Springs, CO 80918 U.S.A.

David C. Cook Distribution Canada
55 Woodslee Avenue, Paris, Ontario, Canada N3L 3E5

David C. Cook U.K., Kingsway Communications
Eastbourne, East Sussex BN23 6NT, England

David C. Cook and the graphic circle C logo
are registered trademarks of Cook Communications Ministries.

The Web site addresses recommended throughout this book are offered as a
resource to you. These Web sites are not intended in any way to be or imply an
endorsement on the part of David C. Cook, nor do we vouch for their content.

All Scripture quotations, unless otherwise noted, are taken from the *Holy Bible,
New International Version*®. *NIV*®. Copyright 1973, 1978, 1984 by International
Bible Society. Used by permission of Zondervan. All rights reserved. Scripture
quotations marked NKJV are taken from the New King James Version.
Copyright © 1982 by Thomas Nelson, Inc. Used by permission. All rights
reserved. The author has added italics to Scripture quotations for emphasis.

LCCN 2010930345
ISBN 978-1-4347-6446-1
eISBN 978-1-4347-0260-9

© 2010 Jim Daly
Published in association with the literary agency of WordServe Literary
Group, Ltd., 10152 S. Knoll Circle, Highlands Ranch, CO 80130.

The Team: Brian Thomasson, Alex Field, Amy Kiechlin,
Sarah Schultz, Caitlyn York, Karen Athen
Cover Design: Rule 29, Justin Ahrens
Cover Image: iStockphoto, royalty-free

Printed in the United States of America
First Edition 2010

2 3 4 5 6 7 8 9 10

090610

Dedication

To Christ who strengthens us. He paid the ransom for our souls. To Him belongs all the glory and honor. And to the countless people, some described in this book, who have been courageous witnesses for Jesus Christ through difficult circumstances. For Him and Him alone!

Contents

Introduction

Several years ago, when I served in the international division of Focus on the Family, I was in Beijing to explore opportunities to expand our work in China. It was the end of my stay, and I was saying good-bye at the airport to a kind Chinese missionary couple who had hosted me for part of my trip. I'd started to move toward the line for boarding my plane when the husband, an earnest man in his thirties, said, "We'll be praying for you."

Normally, my response to a message like that would be, "I'll pray for you, too." And I would mean it. But for some reason on this day, the Lord prompted me to say something different. I stopped, shifted the bag on my shoulder, and asked, "How *do* you pray for us?"

The husband hesitated, glanced at his wife, and then turned back to me. I could see he was struggling to find the right words to answer me.

"Well," he finally said, "we are praying ... for the church in America to get more persecution." He smiled to show he meant no offense. "You see, we see you as rather weak."

On my flight home, I had many hours to think about this man's statement. He, and obviously others viewing the United States from the outside, believes that we in the U.S. church are weak, no doubt in both our faith and our deeds. To counter our weakness, we need strength. And their solution to give us that strength is to pray for persecution to land on our doorstep.

That's not what our prayers are usually about, I thought. *We pray for the gospel to reach far and wide. We ask for protection for our families and loved ones. We seek deliverance from trials. And yes, we ask God for strength to get through the hard times. But pray for persecution?*

The more I thought about it, however, the more I realized that my missionary friend was on to something. In my various roles at Focus on the Family, most recently as president, I have come into contact with many, many hurting people in the United States and around the world. These men and women are struggling. They feel distressed, useless, and vulnerable. Some of the most devastated of all are Christians. They gave their hearts to Christ and anticipated a better life. But instead they discovered trial and pain.

You might be one of them.

Yet in my travels I have also encountered another group of Christian men, women, and children. They, too, face trauma and heartache, yet they are not overwhelmed. You could even say that they embrace their pain. Though the anguish is just as real to them, their ability to cope is radically different. At a point of incalculable weakness, somehow they tap into a new power that lifts them beyond where they started.

They are growing *stronger*.

My conversation with the missionary that day in Beijing led me to reflect on the relationship between troubles, weakness, and strength in God's sovereign plan. I began to wonder: Are the discouraged and brokenhearted actually the people who are closest to discovering joy and power in the Lord? Is great weakness the essential ingredient to discovering great strength? Have we missed this message somehow? Is this a wonderful gift that the Lord is holding out to every nation, to every church, to every individual? To me?

And maybe to you, too?

In the pages ahead, we will take a look at real strength—what it is, what it isn't, and what God says about it. I think you'll be encouraged. The Lord does not waste our frustrations and our tears. I believe that when we let Him, He uses our pain and failures and weakness for incredible good—for ourselves and for His glory.

I hope you'll join me.

Jim Daly
www.JimDalyBlog.com

PART 1

Chapter 1

When I Am Weak

This isn't how it works in the movies.

On a chilly Sunday morning in December, David Works and his family—his wife, Marie, and daughters Stephanie, Laurie, Rachel, and Grace—finish worshipping at New Life Church in Colorado Springs. As usual, they stay after the service to enjoy conversation with friends. On their way to the exit, David announces that lunch will be at a nearby hamburger restaurant called Good Times. The members of the Works family pull their coats tighter and step into a brisk breeze, shuffling carefully across patches of snow in the parking lot.

As the family approaches its white Toyota Sienna van, Laurie heads for the left-side sliding door.

"No, no—you have to sit in the back on the other side," Rachel says.

It is a Works family tradition that everyone keeps the same seat for both parts of a trip. Laurie rode to church in the rear right seat of the van, and Rachel intends to continue the custom.

"Okay, okay," Laurie says.

She walks around the back of the van, enters through the right-side sliding door, and takes her place in the back seat. Rachel, behind Laurie, pauses in front of the open right-side door to look for something in her purse.

That is when it starts.

David, sitting in the front passenger seat and in the process of buckling his seat belt, hears a sharp metallic sound. *What was that?* He lets go of the seat belt and swivels his head to the right, surveying the parking lot. To his shock, a young man dressed in black stands just twenty yards away. He's pointing a large assault rifle at the Toyota.

What in the world?

Another shot rings out.

"Get down! Get down! There's a shooter out there! He's shooting at us!" David screams. He curls up in the van's footwell, trying to get as low as possible. He hears the sound of more gunshots mixed with his family's screams. The sound of the shots changes; David understands the shooter is on the move.

Wait a minute—where is Rachel?

She'd been just outside the van when the shooting started. David twists to look behind him. His sixteen-year-old daughter is still standing next to the Toyota, a dazed look on her face. Her burnt-orange T-shirt has a hole in it at the level of her lower-right rib cage.

"Rachel!" David cries.

"I think I've been shot," Rachel says. Suddenly, she collapses, falling backward onto the blacktop.

David jerks his door handle and jumps out. The instant his feet hit the ground, another volley of bullets whizz past his head. He turns; the gunman is no more than ten yards away, rifle pointed directly at him. Before he can move, David feels pain on his right side, just above his waist. He too falls to the pavement. The shots continue.

"Gracie, get down and play dead! He's still here!" David orders. His youngest daughter, eleven years old, had been moving from the backseat to help her sister.

The firing stops momentarily, then resumes, but the sound is more distant and muffled. David realizes the gunman has gone into the church.

David has been shot in the abdomen and groin. He stretches his arm in Rachel's direction, willing his body to move. His daughter needs her father—*her protector*—yet David can't even crawl. Through tears, he says, "I'm so sorry, honey. I can't reach you."

"That's okay, Daddy," Rachel whispers.[1]

On this horrifying, heartwrenching day, David Works would give anything to turn into a Hollywood action hero. If this were a movie, he would be Superman, leaping in front of his daughter and watching bullets bounce harmlessly off his chest. With his super strength, he would pick up the van and fly his family to safety, then return to catch the bad guy before he could hurt anyone else.

But this isn't a movie.

David Works has no super strength. He is lying in a church parking lot, weak, helpless, and bleeding, and watching the life ebb from his beloved daughter.

Panic Attacks

Let's leave this traumatic scene for the moment and visit the mother of a different family. Lori Mangrum is a pastor's wife. She and her husband, John, have two children. But Lori isn't thinking about her family right now. She's slumped in a chair at home. The curtains are drawn. For months, she hasn't slept or eaten well.

Lori grew up in a Christian home and learned to smile and appear joyful no matter what was going on around her. Like any family, she and her parents and siblings had their share of troubles, but Lori didn't want to burden her parents with her own fears and worries. She became the "sunshine" for her family, always working to cheer up others but rarely addressing her own emotional needs.

Years later, after marrying John, having kids, and moving to a new home, Lori started experiencing panic attacks. Without warning, feelings of terror overwhelmed her. She felt a crushing weight in her chest and became nauseous, dizzy, and disoriented. She thought she would die. The attacks increased to the point that Lori couldn't drive a car or go into a grocery store.

One day, after a series of tests, a physician explained to Lori that she had a benign heart condition that could cause some of the symptoms of panic attacks. *Finally!* Lori thought. *I knew they would find something!*

But the doctor wasn't finished.

"You have another problem," he said gently. "I believe this problem manifested itself because of some psychological problems. I want you to see a psychiatrist."

Lori couldn't believe it. *I don't have any stress,* she told herself, *and what stress I do have I handle better than many others!*

Now, sitting in the dark at home for week upon week, Lori is depressed. Friends have told her, "Pray harder, get yourself together, and stop this!" Yet she doesn't even have the energy to talk, eat, or take a shower. Lori is disgusted with herself. She would give anything to change her circumstances, but emotionally, she feels weak and helpless.[2]

Those Uncomfortable Feelings

You may never have faced a crazed gunman or dealt with debilitating depression, but I'm guessing that at some point in life—perhaps many times—you've experienced some of the same feelings that David Works and Lori Mangrum went through in the incidents described above.

Weak. Helpless. Useless. Vulnerable.

Some pretty uncomfortable feelings, right?

We all do our best to avoid situations that expose our failings and fragility. But whether it's a life-or-death crisis or the challenge of simply getting through another day, sooner or later we each confront the undesired sense of being powerless, worthless, feeble, disabled, and dependent on others.

And we don't like it.

Most of us, especially in America, grow up with the idea that we can shape our own destinies. This, after all, is the land of opportunity. This is a place where dreams come true. We see ourselves as rugged individualists, fully capable of taking control of our lives and rising to the top.

And the weak? "Those people" are not us. Most of us profess to have empathy for the struggling and more helpless members of our society. But many of us are also conditioned to feel, deep down, a certain amount of disdain for the unfortunate few. You're homeless? That's too bad—but maybe you need to work harder at finding a job. You're depressed? Yeah, I get discouraged sometimes too—but enough of feeling sorry for yourself; it's time to get yourself together.

Part of the problem is that the weak and helpless are all around us, and when we see others having problems, it reminds us that we're vulnerable too. Some of us cope by closing our eyes and shutting our ears to troubles. I will confess that this can be my attitude at times. But no matter how hard we try to ignore the trials of others, they rise to our attention like steam from a teapot. We think we've guarded our minds and hearts, and suddenly we're faced with:

- The distraught mother who watches her teenage son storm out of the house in anger, not knowing what to say or do and wondering when or if she'll see him again.
- The discouraged father of four who has lost his job, has been evicted from their home, and is so deeply in debt that he doesn't see a way out.
- The terrified little girl who is sexually molested by her "uncle" when Mom isn't home and is told to keep quiet about it "or else."
- The lonely wife who thought she was marrying a soul mate and is desperate because she can't get her husband to talk to her.
- The sullen fourth-grader who repeatedly gets teased and bullied by a sixth-grader on the way home from school.
- The worried single mom whose son is being recruited by a neighborhood gang.

- The shocked fifty-year-old who has just been diagnosed with terminal cancer.
- The young woman who feels paralyzed by depression and guilt over an abortion.
- The husband who can't forgive himself for an affair.
- The despairing grandmother who is watching her children and grandchildren destroy their lives with alcohol and drugs, yet doesn't know what to do about it.

It's hard enough to put aside the struggles and weaknesses of family, friends, coworkers, and neighbors. It's harder still when the hurting wife, husband, mother, father, little girl, young man, or grandmother is *us*.

Do you know what I'm talking about? Are there times when you feel utterly incapable of dealing with the skyscraper-sized obstacle in your path? When you wish you didn't feel more helpless than a bug on your back? When you wish you were Superman or Wonder Woman instead of plain old pint-sized "me"?

If so, I understand at least some of what you're experiencing. One of my earliest memories, from when I was four years old, is of a man suddenly bursting through our front door one night as my brothers and sisters and I were watching TV. The man looked like a monster. His eyes were puffy, red, and glassy. His face was unshaven. He carried an oak-handled, ball-peen hammer in one hand and a jug of Gallo burgundy wine in the other.

The half man, half monster was my father, and he was looking for my mother. When he realized she wasn't there, he roared, "This is what I'm going to do to your mother!" He swung the hammer and bashed a giant hole in the wall. I spent the rest of that night in my bedroom, cowering under a blanket, even after the police arrived and took my dad away.

Up to that point, I'd enjoyed a fairly typical childhood. I was more worried about missing favorite TV shows like *Batman* than whether I would make it to the age of five. But everything changed for me that night. Although I couldn't have put it into words at the time, I suddenly learned just how vulnerable and helpless I really was.

It was a pretty awful feeling.

The feeling grew worse when my parents got divorced, Mom remarried, and we moved to an apartment complex in Compton, California. One night soon after, someone was murdered ten feet away from my ground-floor bedroom window. The rumor was that the killer used a shotgun. Knowing that only four inches of stucco and drywall separated me from whatever was out there left me distinctly scared.

I felt exposed. Defenseless. *Weak*.

The final blow occurred the next year. I understood that my mom was sick. She seemed to get more and more tired and eventually stayed in bed all the time. My stepfather, Hank, was so overprotective that he wouldn't even let us kids talk to her. Weeks later, when my mom went to the hospital, I still just thought she was really sick. It never occurred to me that she might be dying. When my brother Mike told me that Mom was dead, I was shocked. I squeezed Mike's arm so hard that I left fingernail marks. In some strange way I felt that hanging onto Mike would keep me from losing my mother.

My dad was out of my life. My stepfather left the family the day of Mom's funeral and had no real interest in or relationship with my siblings and me. My mother was gone. I felt completely alone—and more helpless than ever.

How I wished it could be different. I wanted something then that I simply did not possess. I wanted *strength*.

A Different Kind of Strength

Most of us admire strength in its many forms. We all want to be strong. But the word *strong* conjures up a variety of meanings and images in our minds. For some, it means sheer physical power. We might think of bulging muscles and the ability to handle the next bad guy who crosses our path. For others, strength is about having the persistence to do what we set out to do—such as taking the lead on a difficult project at work or potty training our children. Some may think of strength of intellect—an ability to outsmart any person or problem. For still others, being strong means appearing immune to any irritations or challenges that threaten to disrupt daily life. Some like the idea of being emotionally detached, to embody a "James Bond" approach to life. Whatever comes up, we'll take care of it, and we'll do it with style.

Think of the figures portrayed so prominently in the media today: politicians such as our current president; technology gurus such as Bill Gates or Steve Jobs; athletes such as Peyton Manning or LeBron James; actors and actresses such as George Clooney or Nicole Kidman; media moguls such as Oprah Winfrey.

Each of these people possesses strengths that the public appreciates. It might be physical strength, emotional strength, talent, intellectual capacity, or influence, but the world admires these folks for what they have that the rest of us don't. They seem to have it together. They appear *strong*.

But I want to talk with you about an entirely different kind of strength. It's a quality of strength that David Works and Lori Mangrum discovered. It is so powerful that it overshadows every other kind of strength, like a Himalayan mountain towering over a molehill. It wasn't the strength that David and Lori were looking for in their moment of crisis, darkness, and greatest weakness. In some ways, it was the furthest thing from their minds. But it was exactly the strength they needed most.

I think it's just what the rest of us need too.

We're Going Through

In the instant after David Works was shot that December day in 2007, he realized he was in a situation that was beyond him. He didn't have the power or strength to control the events around him. He was helpless to protect himself or his family. So he turned to the only one left who did have the power and strength to change matters.

God, what's going on here? he thought. *This is crazy. We're supposed to be a missionary family getting ready to go around the world for You. What's this all about? It doesn't make any sense.*

David sensed an immediate answer. It wasn't audible, but it left a deep impression on him nevertheless: *We're going THROUGH. We're not going OVER or going AROUND this. We're going THROUGH.*

Most of us would be thrilled to receive a message from the Lord. Under the circumstances, however, that message wasn't what David wanted to hear.

David survived the attack on his life that morning. His daughter Rachel and his oldest daughter, eighteen-year-old Stephanie, did not. Stephanie was struck by a bullet while sitting in one of the van's middle seats. She died at the scene. Rachel died a few hours later at the same Colorado Springs hospital where David was treated. The gunman was a twenty-four-year-old who had also killed two people earlier that day at another ministry facility. Inside New Life Church, he'd been shot dead by a security guard before he could claim any more victims.

As the father of two boys, I can only imagine the physical and emotional anguish that David and his family endured in the hours, days, and weeks that followed the shooting and loss of two precious daughters and sisters. I can also imagine that they would have been tempted to curse God for what occurred that day, even to turn away from Him for apparently not intervening when they needed Him most. But that's not what happened.

That first night, lying alone in a hospital bed, overwhelmed by shock and grief, David tried to make sense of the tragedy. He took it straight to God.

Lord, I don't understand You at all right now. I don't get it. How could we lose two kids in one day? You're not making any sense.

But somehow, I trust You in this situation. Obviously I don't have any better ideas. I'm not going anywhere. I will stick with You, Lord, because You have the words of eternal life. I need You tonight more than ever.

From that humble beginning, David found a strength he didn't know he had. After just nine days, he was discharged from the hospital. Gradually, and with persistent effort, he recovered from his physical wounds.

What is more incredible was David's emotional and spiritual recovery. At times the grief and despair overwhelmed him; at one point he was out of control, thrashing, wailing, and sobbing until his voice was hoarse. Yet he was able to attend his daughters' burial and memorial service, where he read the Twenty-third Psalm and thanked God for allowing him to heal quickly enough to be there. A few days after Christmas, he addressed a crowd of 350 people and talked about how, through the nightmare of the previous three weeks, God had never left his family.

Most amazing was that when the New Life pastor asked if David and his family would like to meet with the parents of the gunman, they took a day to think about it, then agreed. And when they met, there was no hesitation. David stretched his arms out and encircled another grieving father and mother in a long embrace, followed by the hugs from the rest of his family. Through tears, he and his family repeated, "It's okay. We forgive you."[3]

Lori Mangrum experienced her own amazing emotional and spiritual renewal. In the midst of her depression, she too turned to God. Though He seemed distant, she began reading Scripture with a new interest and curiosity. She read about the Lord's relationships with sinful men and women and saw how He loved them despite their weaknesses.

One afternoon, while driving home from a session with a therapist, Lori cried out to God, "I can't do this alone. It's too hard. If You're really there, then show me, and I will trust You!"

Lori sensed an answer in the stillness.

Trust Me first—then I will show you.

Starting with small steps, Lori began to relinquish control of her life to the Lord. She focused more on pleasing Him instead of everyone else. It helped her to say no to some requests—and to speak up when she felt upset, angry, hurt, or scared. She began sharing her fears and feelings with her husband. And when a panic attack did strike, she faced it head-on, reassuring herself that she didn't have to cooperate with what her body was trying to tell her.[4]

The grace and courage demonstrated by David Works and Lori Mangrum blows me away. Could I have faced and forgiven the parents of a man who murdered my children? Honestly, I don't know, and I don't want to find out. Could I take the brave steps to surrender to the Lord and allow Him to lift me out of a disabling depression? Again, I'm not sure, and I'd prefer not to take that test.

But am I attracted to what David and Lori have? You'd better believe it. Because what they have demonstrated is not simply physical, emotional, or intellectual strength. It's something far deeper, far more powerful, and far more lasting.

Something spiritual.

Something holy.

David and Lori took the worst that life could throw at them. Did it hurt? *Of course.* Did it bring them to their knees, both figuratively and literally? *Yes.* Did they find themselves utterly weak and helpless? *Absolutely.*

Yet somehow, through that weakness and their connection to a merciful God, David and Lori were transformed. They didn't just survive. They didn't just "get by."

They got *stronger*.

That's the kind of strength I want: a strength that never leaves, a strength that actually magnifies during the tough times, a strength that isn't dependent on me but resides in a power that can't be stopped.

How about you?

I don't presume to have all the answers to life. But I know who does, and I know who provides the greatest strength of all. It is a strength that I believe is found and forged *only* through weakness. It's what the apostle Paul meant in his message to the members of the fledgling Corinthian church: "For when I am weak, then I am strong" (2 Cor. 12:10).

Let's talk about it.

Chapter 2

Double, Double Toil and Trouble

Sometimes the simplest things don't go quite the way we plan. Just ask Amy Tracy.

On a warm Saturday afternoon in Colorado Springs, Amy calmly waited in line for an automated car wash, enjoying the sunshine and the tunes playing on the radio in her Volkswagen Golf. She didn't usually worry much about keeping her vehicle clean. She'd never been to this particular car wash. But she'd just bought the Golf, and she wanted to preserve its fresh, "new car" look.

Amy didn't mind the wait. It was, after all, a beautiful day. When she reached the front of the line, however, she frowned. Ahead of her was a narrow metal track that led into the car wash. She just wasn't sure she could steer her tires into that tiny space.

Amy looked in the mirror. A long line of cars waited behind her. There was no room to back out. Reluctantly, she pulled forward. *Thump!* Her fear was realized—the left front wheel had slipped off the track.

Before Amy could pull out and try again, the garage doors closed in front and back. She was trapped in darkness. Sprayer jets moved into position, blasting her car with water. But the car was out of position, so the front left sprayer began banging against the car.

A feeling of panic engulfed Amy.

No, no! I'm ruining my new car. It's not even paid for!

She tried to back up, but the car wouldn't budge. She was stuck.

How am I going to fix this? Help!

Amy felt the track sliding forward to the next section of the car wash, but her car still didn't move. The sprayer continued to whack at her expensive new vehicle.

She took a deep breath.

I've got to stop this somehow.

Amy opened the door of the Volkswagen and stepped out. Immediately, a heavy mist—a combination of water and soap—washed over her. Her glasses fogged, making it impossible to see. Like a blind person, Amy felt along the wall, searching for the exit. Behind her, the sprayer continued to attack her Golf.

There's got to be a door here somewhere, Amy thought, *or at least a window I can crawl out of.*

Finally, Amy felt a doorknob, turned it, and stumbled into sunlight. She ran to the front of the car wash and waved her arms at the drivers waiting in line, flinging soap and water in every direction. "It's broken! Go home!"

Then she ran over to the car wash attendant.

"You've gotta stop it! The car wash is broken! My car's stuck in there! It's hitting my car!"

The attendant looked at Amy, still flailing her arms and dripping wet, as if she were from outer space. Then he slowly walked over to a machine and hit the "stop" button. Amy eventually limped home in her Golf, relieved to escape the clutches of the malevolent car wash.[1]

Have you ever had one of those days where nothing seems to go your way? The truth is that it happens to us all the time, and we really don't like it. We much prefer comfort and convenience to toil and trouble. In fact, in America especially, we often demand it. We can be sitting in our leather-upholstered vehicle listening to our favorite song on the CD player, the air conditioner tuned to a perfect seventy-two degrees, yet we're tapping our foot with impatience because the fast-food dinner we ordered four minutes ago *still* hasn't arrived.

The expectation that any level of physical or emotional discomfort should be removed from life permeates our society. Think about elevators, escalators, and battery-heated slippers. Consider the millions spent every year on alcohol, drugs, and pain and sleep medications. And then there is the story I heard on the radio about the federal Occupational Safety and Health Administration (OSHA) stepping up its oversight of internship programs because a high school girl working at a law firm experienced paper cuts.

Don't get me wrong—I'm not against OSHA, and I often ride in elevators. I am concerned, however, about what seems an obsession with pursuing comfort at any cost. I am concerned about the idea that strife and pain are symptoms of a disease that has to be stamped out. This approach to life has a dark side. And for many of us, it's an attitude that infects not only our daily lives but also our faith.

For many believers, this is a typical story: They struggle in life. The struggle leads them to an answer to their pain—a personal relationship with Jesus Christ. They move to a level of joy, peace, and fulfillment they've never experienced before. But over time—when life continues to throw them one curve after another—the sense of joy and satisfaction diminishes. They began to doubt their faith, asking questions such as "Lord, where are You? Why are You allowing troubles to bombard me one after another? Surely this isn't the wonderful plan You have for my life?" They continue to go through the motions of attending church, but their hearts are no longer in it. Or they give up their faith altogether.

I can understand many of these feelings. My early life, as I alluded to in the first chapter, was far from ideal. In many ways I think I'm fortunate I even lived through it. We rarely went to church as a family and didn't own a Bible, so my notion of God was pretty fuzzy. Yet the Lord placed some people in my life who gave me the spiritual direction I desperately needed. The first of those were a neighborhood couple we "adopted" as grandparents—Grandma and Grandpa Hope. They led my mom to the Lord Jesus in the hospital just hours before she died.

Then there was Paul Moro—"Coach Mo" to my friends and me. He was my high school football coach and a man of strong Christian faith. During one of our conversations about God, he invited me to a football camp sponsored by the Fellowship of Christian Athletes. That's where I realized that something was missing from my life, something that not even a "normal" family could have provided. One evening at the camp, I stood up in front of a room full of macho high school athletes and asked Jesus to forgive my sins and come into my heart.

Because of what I'd been through, I didn't really expect my life to suddenly turn to ease and bliss—and it didn't. I did find, however, that I had a new sense of hope. I sensed that Jesus was there and ready to walk with me into my future.

As I've talked with other believers, I've discovered that my experience may have been an exception. Many new Christians, either consciously or unconsciously, expect problems to melt away like butter in a frying pan after they give their lives to Christ. Their hearts are transformed, so they figure the world around them should change too.

But it doesn't seem to work that way, does it? If anything, life seems to get even tougher after our spiritual conversion. Which leaves some of us feeling that God has turned His back on us or even betrayed us. Unfortunately, however, that's not really fair to God. You see, He warned us. It's right there in Scripture, in Jesus' words to the disciples: "In this world you will have trouble" (John 16:33). It doesn't say, "In this world your troubles are over." Not even close. No, Jesus *promises* trouble even to His closest followers, to those who have given up everything for Him.

The apostle Paul was equally specific. He told persecuted believers in Thessalonica to not be "unsettled by these trials. You know quite well that we were destined for them" (1 Thess. 3:3). And Paul wrote to Timothy, "Everyone who wants to live a godly life in Christ Jesus will be persecuted" (2 Tim. 3:12).

What do we do with intimidating statements like these? What does this mean for you and me?

I think we're being told that we can't run away from God's design. Pain is part of the plan.

Faith and Persecution

After the resurrection, the disciples clearly remembered Jesus' words and understood that suffering and sacrifice might be in their future. All of them except for John paid for their outspoken faith with their lives:

> Matthew was killed by a sword in Ethiopia; Mark died after being dragged by horses through the streets of Alexandria, Egypt; Luke was hanged in Greece; Peter was crucified upside down; James the Just (half brother of Jesus) was clubbed to death in Jerusalem; James the son of Zebedee was beheaded by Herod Agrippa I in Jerusalem; Bartholomew was beaten to death in Turkey; Andrew was crucified on an X-shaped cross in Greece; Thomas was reportedly stabbed to death in India; Jude was killed with arrows; Matthias, successor to Judas, was stoned and then beheaded.[2]

The disciples were hardly alone in their suffering. Stephen was stoned to death in Jerusalem for accusing the Sanhedrin of murdering Jesus. Paul was beheaded in Rome. Barnabas was stoned to death at Salamis. Thousands more were martyred during the church's first three hundred years for refusing to honor pagan gods or goddesses, for refusing to call the Roman emperor "Lord," and for refusing to denounce Christ.

The methods of the Romans were brutal. Nero, emperor from AD 54 to 68, was said to be especially sadistic when it came to executing Christians: "Mockery of every sort was added to their deaths. Covered with skin of beasts, they were torn by dogs and perished, were nailed to crosses, or were doomed to the flames and burnt to serve as nightly illumination."[3]

Any of these people could have rejected their faith in Christ and saved their earthly lives. They weren't stupid. They saw what was happening to the believers around them and knew they were at risk every moment of the day. Yet they chose to stay faithful and endured grisly deaths. Why? The obvious answer is that their faith was genuine. They believed at the core that a better, eternal life awaited them, and they would do or undergo anything to possess that life.

I believe there is also a second reason for their incredible steadfastness in the face of torture and death: They understood at some level that sacrifice is necessary to follow Christ; that the Lord responds to us when we suffer for Him. It draws us nearer to Him, and when we do so, He gives us the strength to go through even the worst of trials.

In the United States, we don't face this kind of persecution for our beliefs. Our experience in this country is nothing like what the early church encountered in the years following Christ's death and resurrection. It is much easier and safer to proclaim our faith. And most of us are glad about that. We're not eager to play the role of victim at the hands of an oppressive regime.

But are we missing something here? Does our "easy" faith prevent us from sending our roots deep into the fertile soil of relationship with the Lord? Did those first-century martyrs have an intensity of belief, a joy and peace, a connection to God's power that we can't quite grasp?

I think my missionary friend in China would say yes. This is why he and others are praying for persecution to come to the American church. He knows that Christianity is growing in China despite efforts to thwart it.[4]

A survey at the time of this writing gives a picture of what Christians are facing around the world right now[5]:

- Three Christians were killed and two others wounded in Kirkuk, Iraq. Attackers slit the throats of a woman and her daughter-in-law, killing them both. In another neighborhood, gunmen attacked a Christian family, killing one boy instantly.

- Two families were driven from their villages in West Java, Indonesia, after they converted from Islam to Christianity.

- The Taliban attacked six churches, burned several Christian homes, and injured children in Karachi, Pakistan. They shouted "Accept Islam!" during the attack.

- Two women were arrested and jailed in Iran for being "antigovernment activists." Both are Christians.

- A Christian pastor in the state of Orissa, India, was dragged from a bus, tortured, and killed by Hindu radicals.

- Three Christians died in a military prison in the African country of Eritrea. At least one of the deaths was the result of torture after the prisoner refused to recant his faith.

- Government officials in North Korea publicly executed a thirty-three-year-old mother of three for distributing the Bible, as well as for other "crimes." Her husband, children, and parents were sent to a political prison.[6]

The persecution of Christians has been with us since the beginning of the church. It is the same today as it was when Jesus spoke directly to His disciples: "If the world hates you, keep in mind that it hated me first. If you belonged to the world, it would love you as its own. As it is, you do not belong to the world, but I have chosen you out of the world. That is why the world hates you" (John 15:18–19).

What I find interesting is that during the first century, when the world expressed its hate by torturing and executing Christians, the church experienced exponential growth. Today, in corners of the world where Christians are persecuted, the church is also thriving. It seems that the harder the world tries to douse the fire of Christianity, the faster it spreads.

Maybe, in the United States and in other nations where our faith encounters less resistance, we're looking at our situation in the wrong light. Maybe instead of thinking of our circumstances as an advantage, we should view them as a disadvantage.

Maybe, as crazy as it sounds, we need to pray for persecution because it will make us stronger.

The Purpose of Our Pain

When Mary Frances Bowley married her high school sweetheart, she had her future planned out. She would be a mother and kindergarten teacher, helping children learn and grow. After a couple of decades she would retire from teaching and enjoy her golden years with her husband.

That wasn't how it worked out. Nine years into what Mary Frances thought was a great marriage, she found out her husband was having an affair. Soon after, he drove off in their paid-for red

Ford truck and left Mary Frances with house payments, car payments, two dogs, and a five-month-old baby.

Mary Frances had gone to church, read God's Word, kept up on her devotions, and led women's Bible studies for years. The Lord had always been part of her life. But it wasn't until her life began to crumble that He became her lifeline. When she began to fervently pursue Him, she discovered a love and a power that she never knew existed. It changed her life. Eventually, the Lord led her to a devoted husband and gave her the passion and strength to launch an Atlanta-based ministry that helps broken women rebuild their lives.[7]

I don't mean to be flippant about the idea of praying for persecution. Far from it. I certainly do not wish divorce on anyone. But I am seeking an answer to the question we all confront sooner or later: *If God is a loving God, why does He allow us to suffer? What is the purpose of our pain?*

When a child touches a hot stove, it burns his finger, and pain receptors send a signal to the brain. He gets the message pretty quickly: *That hurts! Don't do that anymore!*

In this case, the purpose of pain is to warn away from doing things that harm our body.

Yet there are many other kinds of pain, as we've already seen. Some kinds of pain we could not possibly anticipate or prevent: an attack by a crazed gunman; the onset of a rare form of cancer. However, pain in the form of persecution that is the direct result of our faith is different. In a sense, we choose that suffering. So what is the purpose in these instances?

I believe that, as is so often the case with Christianity, the Lord turns what at first seems logical to us on its head. Our pain, suffering, and weakness are not so much conditions to avoid or endure, as conditions to cherish. They benefit us in ways we cannot see at the time. Even more important, they accomplish *His* purposes.

Let's see how this applies to Paul. We know that he suffered as he worked to spread the gospel message during the first century. He describes it himself:

> Five times I received from the Jews forty lashes minus one. Three times I was beaten with rods, once I was stoned, three times I was shipwrecked, I spent a night and a day in the open sea, I have been constantly on the move. I have been in danger from rivers, in danger from bandits, in danger from my own countrymen, in danger from Gentiles; in danger in the city, in danger in the country, in danger at sea; and in danger from false brothers. I have labored and toiled and have often gone without sleep; I have known hunger and thirst and have often gone without food; I have been cold and naked. (2 Cor. 11:24–27)

Is Paul complaining here? Not at all. He is describing his own weaknesses—boasting about them, as he puts it (v. 30)—in order to contrast them with the Lord's power. In fact, Paul views suffering for Christ as a gift. He writes to the believers at Philippi, "For it has been granted to you on behalf of Christ not only to believe on him, but also to suffer for him" (Phil. 1:29). The Greek word used here for *granted* means "freely given." In other words, it is a gift and privilege to suffer for Jesus this way.

That may still be a pretty tough concept to wrap our minds around—that suffering for Christ is a gift from the Lord. I know it is for me. But perhaps it begins to make more sense when we read how Paul relates some of the personal benefits of this gift to the Corinthians:

> To keep me from becoming conceited because of these surpassingly great revelations, there was given me a thorn in my flesh, a messenger of Satan, to torment me. Three times I pleaded with the Lord to take it away from me. But he said to me, "My grace is sufficient for you, for my power is made perfect in weakness." Therefore I will boast all the more gladly about my weaknesses, so that Christ's power may rest on me. That is why, for Christ's sake, I delight in weaknesses, in insults, in hardships, in persecutions, in difficulties. For when I am weak, then I am strong. (2 Cor. 12:7–10)

Paul is saying that this "thorn" in his flesh kept him from being conceited. We don't know the exact nature of this malady. It could have been malaria, epilepsy, a speech disability, or even migraine headaches. Whatever it was, it was a constant reminder to Paul that even though Jesus had appeared personally to him and given him a mission, Paul was not to think too highly of himself. Paul's affliction—*his pain*—was a check against pride. That's a good thing.

Like most of us when we first encounter a trial, Paul didn't recognize this gift right away. As you or I would probably do, he asked for it to be removed—three times. Yet the Lord responded that His grace was all Paul needed. That was huge. In this trial or any other, God was enough. From this single "thorn," Paul learned to renew and deepen his dependence on God. That's also a good thing.

Paul also discovered that the Lord's power is perfected in our weakness. This means that in some mysterious way, God's power is even more potent when we are at our weakest. I think it has to do with us getting out of His way. We don't try to manipulate the Lord's strength once we feel His presence. We are so undone that we allow Him complete control, which naturally (yet often to our surprise) works to our greatest advantage.

Finally, Paul was able to *delight* in his weakness and trials. Delight implies a deep joy, as well as peace and fulfillment. It's not just a passing sense of pleasure, the kind of good feeling that comes from chewing on a chocolate bar, but something far more meaningful and lasting. Isn't that what we all want more than anything—to be fully immersed in the permanent state of meaningful delight that comes from relationship with Jesus?

This is what I mean when I say "God turns everything on its head." As strange as it sounds, Paul discovered this deep delight "in weaknesses, in insults, in hardships, in persecutions, in difficulties" (2 Cor. 12:10).

These are the gifts that made him strong.

Bless You, Prison!

Aleksandr Solzhenitsyn, the famous Soviet writer who spent eight years in forced labor camps and was later exiled from his home country, described his own reasons for viewing suffering as a gift.

It was granted to me to carry away from my prison years on my bent back, which nearly broke beneath its load, this essential experience: how a human being becomes evil and how good. In the intoxication of youthful successes I had felt myself to be infallible, and was therefore cruel. In the surfeit of power I was a murderer and an oppressor. In my most evil moments I was convinced that I was doing good, and I was well supplied with systematic arguments. It was only when I lay there on rotting prison straw that I sensed within myself the first stirrings of good. Gradually it was disclosed to me that the line separating good from evil passes not through states, nor between classes, nor between political parties either—but right through every human heart—and through all human hearts.... That is why I turn back to the years of my imprisonment and say, sometimes to the astonishment of those about me: "Bless you, prison!" ... I nourished my soul there, and I say without hesitation: "Bless you, prison, for having been in my life!"[8]

When Solzhenitsyn was at his weakest and most vulnerable, he discovered a kind of clarity about the true nature of good and evil. It nourished his soul. It allowed him to see his suffering not just as a terrible detour, but as a blessing. There was a purpose for his pain.

Pastor and theologian John Piper has put it this way:

This is God's universal purpose for all Christian suffering: more contentment in God and less satisfaction in the world. I have never heard anyone say, "The really deep lessons of life have come through times of ease and comfort." But I have heard strong saints say, "Every significant advance I have ever made in grasping the depths of God's love and growing deep with Him has come through suffering."[9]

We've been talking about the benefits that God grants to each of us as individuals in our times of trial and suffering. But I believe there is another purpose for our pain, one that makes our own personal gains pale in comparison. Quite simply, when we are at our weakest and we begin to grow in faith and strength, we display the power of Christ to the world. His light shines brightest when we are nothing. Our faith magnifies His glory.

A few years ago, His glory shone through at a hotel in Ocean City, New Jersey. The innkeeper, a woman named Joyce, took a call from a friend and booked a room for the friend's son, Dennis, and his wife, Michele. The couple did not come to Ocean City to enjoy a carefree vacation, however. They were recovering from an emotionally devastating event.

For years, Dennis and Michele had been trying to have a child, without success. They finally chose to adopt. They'd received custody of a precious baby named Seth. He was everything they'd hoped for. They were overjoyed and looked forward to all the excitement and challenges of parenting.

Then, nearly four months later, they were told that the signature of Seth's biological father had been forged on the adoption documents. The father was now aware that he had a son and wanted to raise Seth himself.

Dennis and Michele were heartbroken, but legally there was nothing they could do. Just before arriving at the hotel, they'd turned over the baby they already loved as their son to a stranger.

Joyce was filled with compassion for the now-childless couple. On the night before their arrival, she tossed and turned in bed and prayed for Dennis and Michele. When they arrived, Joyce saw the grief in their eyes and kept her check-in instructions as brief and businesslike as possible. After showing them to their room, Joyce broke down in sobs.

Later, Joyce wondered if she'd done the right thing by not mentioning Seth. She decided to write a note, which she slipped under the couple's door. It read: "Dear Dennis and Michele: We just want you to know that we love you. Our prayers are with you during this difficult time. If you need a hug or someone to talk to, we are here for you. Love in Christ, the Logan Staff."

Every day of their stay, Dennis and Michele sat on wicker chairs on the hotel's front porch and read their Bibles. When they checked out after four days, they thanked Joyce for the note and shared about how they were coping. To Joyce, it was a revelation.

"We aren't mad at God," Michele said. "We are just so thankful that we could have Seth for four wonderful months. We may have held him in our arms for only a short time, but we'll carry him in our hearts forever."

"We don't understand how it will happen, but we know God will bring good out of it somehow," Dennis added.

Joyce could hardly believe it. She had so wanted to comfort this couple in their grief and pain. Instead, she found herself encouraged and her own faith deepened. In their trial, Dennis and Michele had found a hidden strength that was on display to everyone around them. They also found a renewed joy about a year later when they adopted a son, Zachary, which means "Jehovah has remembered."[10]

Paul said, "For when I am weak, then I am strong" (2 Cor. 12:10). That is true of him as an individual. It is also true of his influence for the Lord. At his most vulnerable point, he was at his strongest as an ambassador for Christ.

In All Things

I know that we've covered some sensitive ground here, and I hope you are encouraged. I firmly believe that any loss or suffering you've experienced is not squandered or for naught. We serve a loving and merciful God. He created us with the gift of freedom of choice, and our bad choices—starting with Adam and Eve—continue to lead to a great deal of pain. But that pain *does* serve a purpose. It benefits us and brings glory to Him: "We know that in all things God works for the good of those who love him, who have been called according to his purpose" (Rom. 8:28).

Pain makes us stronger.

In the chapters ahead, we'll talk more about the issues we've raised here. We will look at a progression that I believe is common to all of us who call ourselves Christians. It is not an easy road, and it challenges us to make an important choice. Yet if we choose wisely, it ends with the wonderful evidence of God's grace: *peace, strength, and hope.*

Chapter 3

The Choice: Beaten, Bitter, or Broken

In 1989, I had a big decision to make.

I'd been working in northern California in the sales division for International Paper, one of the industry leaders in the field of paper and packaging products. On a Wednesday night, the plant manager took me to dinner at a French restaurant in Berkeley, where he offered me an upper-management position with a six-figure salary. I enjoyed working at IP and was excited about the opportunity. I was also pleased that it would give me the financial means to take care of my wife, Jean, and the children we hoped to raise. We could even buy our first house.

"I'll give you until Monday to make your decision," the manager said. Then he winked. "But I already know what it's going to be."

I got home that night and told Jean the whole story. We both were enthusiastic about this new direction for us. A few minutes later, Jean said, "By the way, there's some kind of business message on the phone for you. You might want to check it out before bed."

The message was from a man named Ron Wilson. Ten months earlier, Ron had talked to me about a potential new position I might be interested in at a nonprofit organization called Focus on the Family. Jean and I admired the Focus mission to strengthen marriages and families and were big fans of Dr. James Dobson's radio broadcasts, so we were intrigued by the opportunity. But the months passed, and I didn't hear back from Ron. I didn't want to force my way into something that wasn't the Lord's will, so we let it go.

But now, Ron's message said the position had finally been approved. *Would I still be interested?*

Suddenly, I had two opportunities to consider. Jean and I discussed and prayed about both options. We knew Focus wouldn't be able to offer the same compensation as International Paper. But money wasn't the only consideration. The Focus mission was close to our hearts and touched thousands of families around the United States and the world. The chance to help families in a godly way and to work with Dr. Dobson and the amazing team at Focus on the Family was more than enticing. In different ways, this also was a very exciting possibility.

I called Ron and flew to Los Angeles the next day for a series of intense interviews and meetings with Dr. Dobson and other Focus executives. Everyone saw this as a fit. Throughout the day and on the flight home, Jean and I continued to talk and pray. When Ron called on Saturday to ask me to join the Focus on the Family team—at one-third the salary I would make at International Paper—I knew what my heart was telling me. Ten minutes later, after one last conversation with Jean, I called Ron and accepted the offer. I've never regretted the decision.

We all make thousands of choices every week. Some are routine, such as deciding what to wear or what to eat for lunch. Some are instinctive; if the sun is too bright, we close our eyes without thinking. Others, like my choice about a job, require measured thought and prayer and have long-range consequences.

And some decisions have even greater impact. These are the choices that change everything about the way we live and how we relate to the Lord.

The question of whether we really make our own decisions is a point of contention in some circles. Many learned men and women have debated for centuries about the nature of God and free will. I don't claim to be a theologian, but it seems to me that the freedom to choose—whether it is to put on a green shirt in the morning or to believe in the Lord and obey His commands—is a gift from our Maker. He does not force us to believe in or follow Him. He is a gentleman that way.

To me, this is the only way that Bible verses like these make sense: "If anyone chooses to do God's will, he will find out whether my teaching comes from God or whether I speak on my own" (John 7:17), and "Whoever is thirsty, let him come; and whoever wishes, let him take the free gift of the water of life" (Rev. 22:17).

With that said, I don't believe God simply allows us to do whatever we will while He sits idly on a mountain, observing us with only casual interest. He strongly desires that we choose to love Him and enter into relationship with Him, and He actively pursues this relationship with us. And although we don't always like it, one of His most effective means of pursuit involves allowing us to confront difficult trials.

Remember Jesus' promise in the last chapter, "In this world you will have trouble" (John 16:33)? Let's look at His statement in the context of the larger passage. The disciples have just told Jesus that they believe He comes from God. Jesus' reply foreshadows His fate on the cross.

> "You believe at last!" Jesus answered. "But a time is
> coming, and has come, when you will be scattered,
> each to his own home. You will leave me all alone.
> Yet I am not alone, for my Father is with me.
>   "I have told you these things, so that in me you
> may have peace. In this world you will have trouble.
> But take heart! I have overcome the world." (John
> 16:31–33)

I cannot help wondering if Jesus' words for the disciples are also a message to all of us. They strike me as a microcosm of what it means to experience the Christian life. Take a look at the progression here and see how it compares to our lives as believers. First, Jesus acknowledges the moment of genuine faith ("You believe"). Second, He describes a time when the disciples—and perhaps the rest of us—will be tested to the point that our faith is shaken. We will be scattered and may be away from Jesus for a time. Jesus knows this is going to happen.

Third, Jesus reminds us that if we choose to remember His words and teaching, we'll understand that this is all part of the plan, and we'll return to Him with renewed faith—as the disciples did—far stronger and more steadfast than before ("in me you may have peace"). Finally, Jesus summarizes everything He's said: You'll experience trouble, but be encouraged, it will drive you to Me and the greatest power.

The hidden key here is that there is a point of major decision, and I'm not talking about the one where we initially give our hearts to the Lord. After we believe and make a commitment to Him, we *will* encounter hardship—enough of it that we may somehow find ourselves distant from God. There's nothing wrong with that by itself. He expects it. What's important is how we ultimately respond to our crisis (or crises), because I believe that's one of the significant turning points of life. Sooner or later, we choose either the road to despair or the path to His power and peace.

You might say that there are three signposts at this fork in the road. Each signpost is an arrow pointing in a different direction. Scratched into the fading wood of each signpost is a single word. To the left is one that reads "Beaten." To the right is a sign marked "Bitter." And down the middle is a sign that says "Broken." Let's journey a ways down each of these paths and explore what they might mean to us.

Burned and Beaten

On April 11, 1974, Brian Shul is a twenty-five-year-old Air Force lieutenant training fighter pilots in advanced combat techniques near the end of the Vietnam War. He also flies covert missions for a special-ops wing of the U.S. government.

Brian has already completed one routine mission when his scheduler asks if he can fit in a quick flight to the Cambodian border. The Special Forces team there needs more cadmium batteries. Brian hesitates; he's tired and ready to go home for the day. But it's a short flight, and he has friends in the Special Forces unit. He agrees to make one last flight.

An hour later, Brian hurtles over the jungle in an AT-28D trainer-turned-fighter. He lowers his altitude for the approach to the border base when suddenly the plane fails to respond to pressure on the throttle.

His heart rate kicks into overdrive. *Well, this isn't good.*

Brian tries every trick he knows to regain control of the plane, but nothing works. What he doesn't know is that Vietcong in the jungle below just shot several rounds of small-arms fire into the AT-28D, severing the link between throttle and engine.

Brian clicks on his radio. "Tiger 18 is declaring an emergency," he says. "I'm not going to make the runway."

Seconds later, the AT-28D makes contact with the top of the jungle canopy. The trees tear at the plane's fuselage and wings, creating an unearthly shrieking sound. Dark, twisted shapes claw for Brian's body as the plane begins to tear. He feels as if he's being ripped apart. The plane drops lower and lower.

Finally, the shrieking, clawing, and slashing stop. All is silent. But Brian feels unbearably hot. Pain seems to scream at him from every inch of his body. He's sitting directly over the fuel pumps, which ignited the moment the plane crashed.

I'm on fire. I've got to get out!

Brian stands, but something yanks him back toward his seat. He can barely see—heat has melted his exterior visor—but he realizes the quick-release microphone cord has melted to his helmet. He grabs the cord with both hands and rips it in half, releasing him from the seat.

Acting on instinct and powered by adrenaline, Brian jumps to the left wing and hurries to the tip. He leaps ten feet to the ground, rolls, gets up, and runs. About a hundred yards away, reeling from pain and shock, he collapses.

An hour passes before the Special Forces unit reaches the crash sight. The first to find Brian is a friend named John. The sight of Brian's charred body causes John to turn away and vomit.

Later, at a naval hospital in Okinawa, doctors tell Brian he's lucky to be alive, that only a young man in peak physical condition could have survived. Brian doesn't feel lucky. Third-degree burns cover his face, neck, arms, hands, thighs, and part of his torso. His body looks like something in a butcher shop. Doctors have inserted long steel pins into each finger to keep his hands from curling into useless appendages.

Every morning, doctors place Brian's naked body into a whirlpool filled with saline solution. At one point, he finds himself surrounded by five hospital technicians armed with scalpels. The technicians perform a procedure known as debridement—the surgical removal of dead and contaminated tissue. In earlier sessions, hospital staff administered the highest possible safe dosage of morphine, but it did nothing to ease Brian's agony, so they gave it up. He endures the treatments without painkillers of any kind. The staff cuts off each treatment after twenty minutes; any longer, and the shock could kill their patient.

Day after relentless day, the torture continues.

Brian has trusted Jesus since childhood, but this isn't what he thought he signed up for. *You may have a plan here, God,* Brian thinks, *but You've got the wrong person. I can't do this. There's no sense going through all this. It's going to kill me. I thought I was tough. I thought I was strong. I admit it—I'm not. Please just let me die.*

Finally, while lying in his hospital bed in the middle of the night, Brian decides he's had enough.

I'll never fly again, he thinks. *No woman will want to date me. I'll never be able to enjoy eating again. I'll never go hiking because I can't be in the sun. I'll never be strong enough to play sports again. Everything that was fun in my life is gone. I'm just a freak. God, I don't want anyone to see me like this. I don't want to live like this. Please let me die.*

Two feet from Brian's head is an IV machine. He focuses on the gray lever that regulates the flow of nutrients keeping him alive.

If I could turn that switch, I could sleep forever.

Brian closes his eyes to concentrate. His bandaged right arm, unsteady, rises an inch, then another. Putting all his energy into lifting his arm, he manages to raise it six inches into the air.

The effort is too much. The arm falls back down. Brian blinks back tears. He is completely beaten and doesn't even have the strength to kill himself.[1]

Is This It?

Can you relate to some of the things Brian Shul felt in that Okinawa hospital? Have you ever felt so overwhelmed with pain or defeated by guilt, anxiety, or hopelessness that you wanted to end it all? Have you ever told God, "You've picked the wrong person. I'm not strong enough. I can't do this"?

I certainly empathize with those feelings. I remember a day when I was so despondent that I couldn't see a purpose for my existence. It was during Thanksgiving break of my sophomore year at California State University San Bernardino. All the other students had gone home for the break, but I had nowhere to go, so I talked school officials into letting me stay alone in the dorm. I recall sitting in my cold and lonely room, feeling hurt and lost, wondering if my life was going anywhere.

I'd given my heart to Jesus, but something huge was still missing. I thought about the loss of my mother and father and everything I'd gone through. The tears began to flow. I prayed, *Lord, is this what life's about? It is just about pain? Is this it?*

Life is hard. Those three words don't do justice to the anguish that sometimes descends on us. For some, the choice to continue, to keep breathing and surviving, is unbearable. More than thirty-three thousand people take their own lives in the United States each year.[2] Each one of those numbers is a testament to indescribable pain and agony, not only for those who are gone, but also for those who are left behind.

I don't want to minimize that kind of pain. If you have experienced it or are going through it now, I realize that telling you to "hang in there" or even to "give it to God" isn't enough. The truth is that nothing I write here will be enough.

While acknowledging that, I still genuinely want to encourage you. There is One who understands what you feel in a way that no one else can. When His tormenters hammered spikes through His flesh, I'm guessing that Jesus did not feel like a heaven-sent Savior. I believe that in some way, in those moments He put His deity aside for us. He experienced the worst of what it's like to be human, when He felt devastating physical and emotional pain and knew what it meant to be utterly rejected and alone. This is why He cried out, "My God, my God, why have you forsaken me?" (Matt. 27:46).

In that moment, perhaps like you and like most of us at one point or another in our lives, Jesus was beaten. But that wasn't the end of His story. And being beaten doesn't have to be the end of your story.

A Bitter Loss

Tom Bowers enjoyed a special relationship with his sister, Margie. Next to his wife, Cathie, Margie was Tom's best friend. They grew up together in Liberia, where their parents served as missionaries and where Tom and Margie shared games, jungle explorations, and their dreams for the future.

On April 29, 1977, Tom, twenty-seven years old, and Margie, twenty-five, live in the United States—Tom in Wheaton, Illinois, and Margie in nearby Oak Park. They talk almost every evening, and this night is no exception. Over the phone, Margie tells Tom how excited she is about her new job. They make plans for Tom to help Margie move into a new apartment the next day.

A few hours later, Tom's phone rings. It isn't Margie this time. It's the police, and the news is devastating.

Margie has been brutally murdered.

The details are like a bad dream to Tom. Margie had just arrived home after an errand. A young man named Thomas Vanda, someone Margie knew casually from his occasional visits to her neighborhood Bible study, wanted to know how to find Esther, Margie's former roommate and classmate.

Margie, perhaps sensing trouble, refused to tell the young man anything. Vanda got angry and suddenly attacked Margie with a hunting knife, stabbing her over and over. A neighbor heard Margie's screams and called the police.

Margie's violent and senseless death is more than Tom can bear. He's filled with anger and a desire for vengeance. A year later, in the courtroom for Vanda's trial, he sits directly behind his sister's murderer. He thinks about how easy it would be to extend his arms and strangle him.

When Vanda is convicted and sentenced—three consecutive life sentences without parole—Tom watches the killer shrug his shoulders and smirk.

Tom seethes inside.

He tries to get on with life, but memories of Margie haunt him. He remembers her love of playing the guitar and singing. He thinks of how much his son would have enjoyed his aunt Margie. At other times, he fantasizes about being with Margie on that fateful night, of ripping the knife out of Vanda's hands and turning it on Vanda himself. His anger becomes so overwhelming that sometimes he feels physically sick.[3]

Tom spirals into the long, dark tunnel called bitterness.

Battery Acid in the Soul

Bitterness is easy to justify and difficult to recognize in ourselves. Maybe that's because it grows and develops over time. It starts when something bad happens, usually something we believe is unjust and undeserved. We feel wounded and hurt. We search for a way to deal with the pain. Sometimes, that leads to a defeating attitude of self-pity.

If we rest in self-pity long enough, it transforms into anger. Our blood pressure rises. We continually replay the incident that caused our pain in the first place. We want to take out our rage on the offender. Often, though, our anger seeps into our relationships with everyone else.

Eventually, our anger descends into the most harmful state of all: *bitterness*. We feel continually distracted by our rage and desire for revenge. We may become discouraged and disillusioned. We find ourselves poisoning our relationships, always blaming others for our problems. We lose our energy, our joy, and our strength. Worst of all, the bitterness we feel blocks us from enjoying a close and vital relationship with the Lord.

Scripture says that "Each heart knows its own bitterness, and no one else can share its joy" (Prov. 14:10). Bitterness is corrosive; it burns to the core. It is like having battery acid in your soul.

Like Tom Bowers, you may have suffered through a period of bitterness in your life. You may be trapped in the throes of bitterness right now. If so, please know that there is a better way. We'll talk about how you can be free of the clutches of anger, hate, and bitterness. If you trust the Lord and allow Him to direct your steps, He will place you on the broken road to peace and strength.

Broken By a Nightmare

Leslie Haskin is head of the operations department for Kemper Insurance Company in New York City. On a Tuesday morning, she is standing by her assistant's desk, getting an update on a problem with a policyholder, when the entire building shakes violently, accompanied by a thunderous noise. Almost instantly, people throughout the office are swearing, crying, and running for the exits. Leslie, however, remains frozen in place.

Leslie stands on the thirty-sixth floor of the North Tower of the World Trade Center. It is September 11, 2001.

Zombielike, Leslie walks into her office and tries to call her cousin, Ronnie. She's not sure why. Maybe it's because he's a smart man and he might be able to explain what's happening. A coworker yells at her to get out of the building, saying "This [expletive] building is coming down." Still numb, Leslie hangs up the phone and finally starts moving.

An explosion forces fire through closed elevator doors. Chilling cries come from the other side of the doors. Leslie and hundreds of others move toward the lone accessible stairwell and cram into the exit single file. The heat is intense, the smell a rancid combination of smoke, chemicals, rusted metal, and burning hair. At one point Leslie and others move to the side to allow a dazed woman and an escort to pass. The woman is burned to the bone; Leslie can actually see ivory and marrow.

On the twentieth floor, Leslie stops for a moment to collect herself. Someone opens a door. A man is standing there, staring, his body oddly crooked and twisted by a column. He has been decapitated.

At last, Leslie reaches the lobby. She is ankle deep in a dark red mixture of water, blood, and jet fuel. The stench is overpowering. Leslie lifts her eyes and prays, *Hear my cry, O God, attend unto my prayer.*

Leslie stumbles outside, where the horror continues. Nearby, dull thuds and the sounds of exploding flesh mark the end of lives; people trapped by fire on the floors above are jumping to their deaths. A fireman gently pushes Leslie forward. "You can't stay here. It's not safe," he says. "Keep moving. *Run.*"

And so Leslie runs. She crosses a sky bridge. She spots Nancy, an old commuter friend. They stop to look at the towers, the smoke and flames, the men and women taking flight and falling, falling. Together, they keep moving. They reach a ferry dock. Nancy pushes her way on, pulling Leslie with her.

As the ferry slowly slips across the water, Leslie looks back at Manhattan Island and the burning towers. As she watches, suddenly, almost gracefully, the South Tower collapses in on itself and disappears from the skyline. It doesn't seem real.

Leslie gets off the ferry at the Hoboken train terminal and says good-bye to Nancy. She boards a commuter train. Hours later, the train finally starts to move. Leslie rides in silence. She gets off at her stop, finds her car, and gets in.

Okay, okay, she thinks. *Which way is home?*

A few minutes later, Leslie pulls into her driveway. Her next-door neighbor and her daughter are talking in front of their house. Leslie calmly gets out of her car and raises her hand as if to wave hello. And there, at that moment in her driveway, when the contrast between normal and nightmare is greatest, the horror and sickness and sadness and pain that have been building up all day inside Leslie finally erupt.

She falls to her knees and screams.[4]

The Hand of the Potter

By the end of the day on September 11, 2001, the person Leslie Haskin used to be no longer existed. The new Leslie could barely function. She boarded her windows with thick wooden shutters to keep "them" out. She put homemade weapons under her bed "just in case." She couldn't go back to work because she couldn't cross bridges, pass through tunnels, get on elevators, or enter high-rise buildings. She had panic attacks when alone and anxiety attacks when surrounded by people. Leslie was diagnosed with post-traumatic stress disorder.

Leslie lost her job, her car, friends who tired of supporting her, and finally, her house. She and her teenage son were homeless for four months.

Leslie was broken. What she eventually realized, however, is that broken—although excruciatingly painful—is sometimes the right place to be.

Scripture tells us that the Lord once said to Jeremiah,

> "Go down to the potter's house, and there I will give you my message." So I [Jeremiah] went down to the potter's house, and I saw him working at the wheel. But the pot he was shaping from the clay was marred in his hands; so the potter formed it into another pot, shaping it as seemed best to him.
>
> Then the word of the LORD came to me: "O house of Israel, can I not do with you as this potter does?" declares the LORD. "Like clay in the hand of the potter, so are you in my hand." (Jer. 18:2–6)

I see a great distinction between beaten, bitter, and broken. When we're beaten, we are in a sense limp and useless. We're like clay that dissolves at a touch. The potter can't do anything with us because we don't hold our shape.

But when we're bitter, we're like a single piece of clay that's grown hard and inflexible. We're equally useless to the potter because we aren't malleable. The shape we're in doesn't do any good to anyone, and the potter can't mold us into a new and better form.

Being broken, however, is a different story. Like Leslie, we may be shattered into pieces, but there is strength in those pieces. When we invite the potter to combine His skill with our strength, little though it might be, He molds us into a new, more useful, and more lasting form—one even stronger than before.

The reality is that choosing to move into brokenness sometimes feels impossible. We can be so overwhelmed that we live in defeat for months or even years before we are able to invite God to work with our broken pieces. Sometimes bitterness rules our thoughts and actions, and it takes a lifetime to work out our escape. Sometimes we bounce back and forth or experience all three. Some of us never escape.

The good news is that God is always with us: "Never will I leave you; never will I forsake you" (Heb. 13:5). He is standing by, always ready to turn on the potter's wheel and gently mold us into the shape we were meant for, if we can just find the will to give Him the chance.

The Broken Path

I'm convinced that even though the Lord chooses not to exercise control over our attitudes and faith, He is continually arranging circumstances that give us the opportunity to choose the broken path to Him.

Let's look again at Leslie Haskin. She grew up in Chicago in a large Christian family. She was raised to respect and obey the Word of God, and she embraced the Christian life. As a teen, however, Leslie was increasingly drawn to worldly measures of success—bright lights, big houses, and fancy cars. She packed away her love for the Lord and instead pursued personal achievements.

Leslie had put God firmly in the backseat of her life by September 11, 2001. But after the tragic events of that day, she realized that running her own life wasn't really working or even possible. She understood that she couldn't go on without her Maker and Savior. Over time, she began to recognize that on 9/11, "I was exactly where I needed to be in order that grace might find me."[5]

Through her horrific experience, Leslie eventually saw that she had a choice to make, and she made it. Months after 9/11, she threw away her medications, acknowledged her brokenness, and gave herself completely to the Lord. Today she is founder and executive director of Safe Hugs, a nonprofit organization providing rehabilitation and healing to women and children who are homeless and victims of domestic violence. More importantly, she is choosing daily to stay broken and therefore moldable by God.

"I believe that God allowed me to choose my life and then He molded the consequences of those choices to bring me closer to Him," Leslie says. "I chose a path that led me to the World Trade Center. He chose the road that led me out. God knew all that it would take to bring me to my knees before Him … in repentance AND in love. He knew exactly what would send me running into His open arms, and it did."[6]

Remember Brian Shul?

Not long after he tried to end his life in the hospital, he watched a French production of the Easter story and crucifixion of Jesus on television. He shuddered as the Roman soldiers hammered nails into Jesus' hands. Brian looked at his own bandaged hands, which still contained steel pins. For the first time, he truly understood the depth of Jesus' sacrifice. Out of love, Christ was willing to undergo anything we might endure, in order to save us.

After two months and thirty-two burn treatments, Brian was transferred from Okinawa to a San Antonio burn center. While there, he refused a medical discharge from the Air Force. A year later, he made his first flight after the accident. Ten years later, he was flying the SR-71 Blackbird spy plane, the world's fastest and highest-flying piloted jet. Brian had moved from beaten to broken.

"God had a plan for my life," Brian says. "I can't take the credit. It's Him, and I'm along for the ride. I'm thankful every day."[7]

Tom Bowers suffered with his anger and bitterness for years. A decade after the murder of his sister, he ran into Esther, Margie's former roommate. As they talked, Tom realized that since the killer had come looking for her, Esther blamed herself for Margie's death.

"Esther," Tom said, "it wasn't your fault. Margie may not be here to forgive you, but I am. I forgive you on her behalf." A few months later, Esther wrote to Tom and told how his forgiveness had allowed her to let go of her guilt.

Not long after that Tom was preparing to teach his adult Sunday school class. The topic that week was forgiveness.

Suddenly, a voice entered his mind: *So you plan to teach about forgiveness? When are you going to forgive?*

Tom had a choice to make. He didn't think he could forgive a monster, but he also realized that rage and bitterness were destroying his life. He prayed for the Lord's help. One day, while praying with his father, he knew it was time. "Thomas Vanda, I forgive you," he said aloud. He repeated the words again and again. "Thomas Vanda, I forgive you."

Immediately, Tom felt the burden he'd carried for so long, finally *lift*. It was replaced by an overwhelming sense of peace.[8]

A Strange Christmas

I made my own choice to give God my broken pieces during my dark days in the dorms. Soon after my low point at Thanksgiving break, I decided to visit the campus counseling center. When the counselor asked, "What's on your heart?" it was all the invitation I needed to start bawling and pouring out the pain I was experiencing. I don't remember a word the counselor said to me the rest of the day. It was the release of that anguish that began to move me out of defeat and toward the Lord again.

A couple of weeks later, on Christmas Day, I was again alone in the dorms. I remember my Christmas dinner was a Mrs. Smith's pie from the vending machine down the hall. This time, however, I didn't feel so alone. I sensed the Lord telling me, "Jim, you're important to Me. Despite everything that's happened in your life, I have a plan for you. Your life can be important—not for what it does for you, but what it does for others."

That evening, I tied on my roller skates and careened up and down the campus's concrete sidewalks. I had the entire place to myself, more than four hundred acres. Yet I wasn't lonely. I knew that the Lord was with me and that in the days and years ahead He would take care of me and find a way to use me for His good purposes.

I actually enjoyed myself that evening. It was one of the strangest Christmases I've ever had—and also one of the best.

I can't emphasize enough that no matter how devastating your circumstances, Jesus understands where you've been and where you are. He is ready to help. If you can turn *everything* in your life over to Him, you will find the hope and peace you seek. I'm not saying it will happen in an instant. It may not happen today, tomorrow, or next week. For a time, you may not sense His presence or any change at all. Yet He is there, nudging you toward the choice that makes all the difference.

PART 2

Chapter 4

Unconditional Surrender

We've been talking about the choice of *brokenness* and how it will lead you to the Lord and His power, strength, and love. I believe it's where we all want and need to be. But maybe you're not convinced. Maybe this whole concept of allowing your life to be shattered into pieces just doesn't sound very appealing. I can understand that! Yet I urge you to keep reading. It could be that you're being influenced by some of the common misconceptions about brokenness.

Let me share what I believe brokenness is *not*:

- Brokenness is not the same as *sadness*. If we are broken before the Lord, it doesn't mean that we are in a constant state of unhappiness or despair. Even when the tears flow, they are as likely to signal joy as sorrow. Do you remember the story of the sinful woman who brought an alabaster jar of perfume to a Pharisee's house? "As she stood behind [Jesus] at his feet weeping, she began to wet his feet with her tears. Then she wiped them with her hair, kissed them and poured perfume on them" (Luke 7:38). This woman was probably a prostitute who had recently heard Jesus preach and had chosen to follow Him. When she suddenly found herself in His presence, she was broken and overcome with emotion. Her tears were not born of dejection but of love, gratitude, and praise.

- If we choose to be broken, it does not mean that we are committing ourselves to a life of *trial and tragedy*. Yes, the Lord often uses troubles to get our attention and point us toward Him. Yet many people go through hard times and remain on the beaten or bitter road. They never make it to broken. On the other hand, it is certainly possible to be broken before God without going through trauma first. And it's equally possible to stay broken when you've moved from past difficulties into a time that is relatively trouble free. Even during those rare times when my life seems to be sailing along smoothly, I never seem to feel entirely comfortable or at ease. Part of that feeling may spring from my chaotic upbringing. But I hope that the primary reason for it is that I'm resting in a state of brokenness. It's a sense that everything can change in an instant but that I can trust God to manage my future. It's a feeling that keeps me humble and a little on edge, yet offers the peace of heaven. It's not necessarily comfortable, but it's where I want to be.

- Brokenness is not about *lowering our self-esteem*. Dr. Dobson has told a story about a woman who once said to him, "God wants me to think of myself as no better than a worm." She seemed to be referring to David's reference to a worm in Psalm 22:6. "I would like to respect myself," the woman continued, "but God could not approve of that kind of pride, could He?"[1] There is a difference between haughty pride and false humility. God does not view us as worthless worms. After all, He created us in His image, and all that He creates is good: "I am fearfully and wonderfully made; your works are wonderful" (Ps. 139:14). I believe, then, that to choose to be genuinely humble and broken does not mean we are less valuable in the Lord's eyes. As faithful followers of Christ, we never give up our place as cherished children of heaven.

If these examples show what brokenness *is not*, then how do we define exactly what brokenness *is*? I think we can find several clues in Psalm 51. David wrote it at one of the most broken points of his life, after his affair with Bathsheba and the confrontation with the prophet Nathan. Let's examine two parts:

> Have mercy on me, O God,
>> according to your unfailing love;
>> according to your great compassion
>> blot out my transgressions.
> Wash away all my iniquity
>> and cleanse me from my sin.
> For I know my transgressions,
>> and my sin is always before me. (Ps. 51:1–3)

You do not delight in sacrifice, or I would bring it;
> you do not take pleasure in burnt offerings.
The sacrifices of God are a broken spirit;
> a broken and contrite heart,
O God, you will not despise. (Ps. 51:16–17)

In the first part of this psalm, David shows genuine humility. He offers no denials and makes no excuses for his behavior. He calls it what it is—*sin*—and asks the Lord to remove it, not because God owes it to him in any way, but because He is merciful and loving.

In the second passage from Psalm 51, David identifies what the Lord is truly looking for from all of us. It's not so much an outward act such as the sacrifice of an animal. It's more about an internal change of attitude. God is most pleased when our spirits and our hearts bow down to His mercy and will. I don't think that means He wants our spirits crushed or desires to see our hearts in anguish. I believe David is saying that the Lord wants our trust. He wants us to submit our spirits and hearts to Him.

The issue for me, and perhaps for many of us, is going the distance in that submission. It's not so hard to submit some of my spirit—my will to do what *I* think is best—to the Lord. When I think about it and pray about it, I realize that He knows best. And often, it's not a struggle to submit my heart—my emotions as I go through each day—to Him. I know, at least when I put my mind to it, that running my feelings through His filter gives me the right perspective to respond to situations.

But to *always* submit heart and spirit to Him, moment after moment, when things are going well *and* when things are falling apart? To submit to Him what means most to me—my family, my dreams for the future? That's another story. That takes courage. It takes commitment. It takes no-holds-barred trust.

You might say that it takes unconditional surrender.

A Lonely War

In July 1945, after the defeat of Germany in Europe and near what would become the end of World War II, the Allied nations issued a proclamation demanding the unconditional surrender of all Japanese armed forces. On September 2, 1945, aboard the *USS Missouri,* Japanese officials signed the surrender documents that formally ended one of the most devastating wars in the world's history.

Not everyone got the surrender message, however. A handful of Japanese soldiers, stranded on remote outposts throughout the Pacific region, carried on their lonely fight. One of these was Second Lieutenant Hiroo Onoda. In 1944 he was sent to Lubang Island in the Philippines with orders to harass the enemy and prevent attacks on the island. When U.S. and Philippine forces landed on the island in 1945, Onoda and three other soldiers took to the hills.

The months and years passed. Each time leaflets and photographs of family members were dropped in the jungle, telling Onoda and his men that the war was over and urging them to surrender, they considered it a hoax. Onoda, a proud soldier, did not believe that Japan could have lost the conflict. He was still at war. He and the other men stole food, burned crops, and killed at least thirty nationals. One of Onoda's soldiers eventually walked away and surrendered. The other two were killed during skirmishes with search parties and the local police.

Incredibly, nearly three decades later, in 1974, a lone Japanese college dropout discovered Onoda hiding out in the Lubang mountains. A few months later, the former student returned to Lubang with Major Yoshimi Taniguchi, Onoda's former commanding officer. There they again found Onoda. Only after Taniguchi read an official order declaring "individuals under the command of the Special Squadron to cease military activities and operations immediately" did Onoda realize he'd been fighting an unnecessary war for almost thirty years.

Onoda later wrote, "Suddenly everything went black…. I felt like a fool for having been so tense and cautious on the way here. Worse than that, what had I been doing for all these years?"[2]

In those life-transforming moments, Hiroo Onoda realized the truth and that he'd wasted years pressing a battle that had already ended. Yet aren't we all a lot like Second Lieutenant Onoda sometimes? We cling to our pride and our instincts and distance ourselves from the truth. We fight a lonely war against God's desires and purposes for our lives, and in the process, we miss out on the joy and peace that He offers. Our actions, whether they involve lying, stealing, greed, adultery, or any manner of sin, show that we're in open rebellion. Some of us, meanwhile, try to hide our resistance. We may talk the lingo and go to church every Sunday, but inside we're still battling to hang on to what we feel are "our" lives.

Our war is hard, but we fight on, week after week, year after year. The alternative—*unconditional surrender to the Lord*—is too frightening to contemplate. Surrender, after all, might change everything.

No Holding Back

Most of us fear God. In many ways, that's a healthy thing. We certainly should respect the power and knowledge of the Creator of the universe: "The LORD delights in those who fear him, who put their hope in his unfailing love" (Ps. 147:11).

Yet we also fear the Lord in another way. We're afraid to give Him complete control of our lives. We're afraid of what He might do with us. We know that He is good and has our best interests at heart, yet the potential for massive change scares us. The unknown, even if it's better than what we know, can be unsettling and intimidating.

So what do we do? We hold back. Instead of immersing ourselves in complete submission to our Maker, we take a few steps toward Him, then back away. We're like little children on a hot summer day at the beach, testing the waves as they roll onto the sand. We wade in and enjoy the cool water as it washes over our feet. The gentle breeze and smell of saltwater beckons us to go deeper, but we sense the power of those crashing big waves. We're not sure about them. So instead of moving forward and enjoying a romp in the ocean, we run back to the safety of the sand.

The problem is that God does not hold back. He is relentless. He is the ocean's tide that keeps coming in, pursuing the very thing that we want to hide and hold back the most. Out of love, He desires our broken spirits and hearts. His aim for us is complete surrender.

As an eighth-grader in Peachtree City, Georgia, a girl named Laura Warner invited Christ into her heart. When she was a senior in college, Laura felt herself being drawn to a life of ministry. She was excited to realize she'd found her calling. She was less excited that same year when, while driving her car, she sensed the Lord telling her she would be going on a mission trip to China. She hated flying. She asked God for a sign to see if her impression was true. She wanted the announcer to be talking about China when she turned on her radio. She punched a button and heard, "Today in Beijing...."

Yet Laura put China out of her mind. Yes, she wanted to follow the Lord. But flying to another continent was asking too much.

A few years later, Laura again felt that God wanted her to go to China. Once more, she resisted. Again, she asked for a sign, this time that He would bring her an application to show that her impression was from Him.

The next day, a woman at the church where Laura worked as a secretary mentioned that she'd left something on Laura's desk that she "might be interested in." Laura knew the woman had been on a number of mission trips. On her desk, Laura found an application form for a Christian program that sent English teachers to China.

Okay, God, Laura thought. *I think I'm starting to get the message.*

Soon after, Laura found herself teaching English to young students in China. She was thrilled that some of her students, after expressing a discreet interest in learning more about Jesus, eventually gave their hearts to Him. Despite these successes, however, Laura's experience in China was devastating. She grew lonely, depressed, and fearful. She suffered from panic attacks. She could barely function. One especially difficult day, she mustered her courage to attempt a trip to get groceries. Every step filled her with dread. She was nearly there, on a street lined with vendors in booths, when the sights, sounds, and smells overwhelmed her. She ran back to her apartment, hurled herself onto her bed, and cried.

After Laura went back to the United States, the fear and anxiety returned, twice as bad as before. A thought entered her mind: *Go downstairs, get a knife, and end it.* She knew this wasn't God speaking to her. It was the Enemy.

Laura sought help. A counselor recommended she go on a vacation with her family. Though unconvinced it would do any good, Laura went to Florida with her parents and checked into an eleventh-floor condominium. She chose a back room. She feared that if she got near a balcony, she might throw herself off.

One night, while alone in her room, Laura tried to make sense of it all. She felt pulled in every direction by God, the Enemy, and her own desire to control her life. The tension was making her crazy.

Lord, what are You doing with me here? she prayed. *I can't seem to do anything. My life is falling apart.*

Once again, Laura felt a response from God, as clear as if it was an audible voice: "Laura, I want you to surrender your emotional state of being to Me."

Surrender my emotions? Laura thought. *Can I really do that? How?*

She thought some more and decided to write out a "contract" in her journal. In bold letters she printed: "I, Laura Warner, do hereby give up the right to my emotional state to my Lord Jesus Christ." She drew a signature line underneath and prepared to sign.

Then she hesitated.

If I sign this contract, she thought, *He could do anything. He could send those people in white coats to take me away and put me in an asylum. Is that what I want?*

Laura shook her head. *I know God works for my good,* she thought. *Even if He puts me away, He knows what He's doing. It would be stupid not to sign.*

As Laura filled in her signature, she felt a sudden and very welcome release.[3]

Laura's struggles did not end on that night. There were still times she had to fight the urge to take personal control of her life and circumstances away from the Lord. Yet from that point on, the panic attacks lessened and a sense of peace grew. The path to a new life of emotional peace was a commitment to surrendering her emotions to God. He eventually led her to join an Atlanta-area ministry as a "coach" for women who are rebuilding their lives.

"I've learned that we really can trust God," Laura says today. "If we surrender everything to Him, He is enough."

Discipline Born of Love

To me, Laura's story is another example of how the Lord continually works in our lives, arranging and working in circumstances in order to give us the opportunity to submit to Him. He is like the government officials who dropped messages and photographs in the jungle for Hiroo Onoda, telling him that he didn't have to fight anymore, that it was time to surrender.

It's so hard, isn't it? Obedience, submission, and surrender go against our stubborn nature. And we are stubborn! In America especially, we're proud of our independence. We celebrate it every Fourth of July. Our independence is a part of our history. Our ancestors fought and died for it. We tend to forget, of course, that part of what those brave men and women fought for was the right to worship

God in the manner of their choosing. They weren't fighting for the right to ignore God's will and authority.

Yet today, that's what many of us end up doing much of the time. We cling to our independence and freedom and self-rule. Like Second Lieutenant Onoda, we keep fighting our war. Like Laura Warner, we resist the obvious signs that point to God's will. Like Paul, we plead for the Lord to remove the thorns in our flesh. Like the disciples, we scatter and abandon our Savior when according to our eyes He appears powerless and thwarted by the world.

And so the waves of trial and trouble keep coming. And since we're so busy running away, we don't see that these waves are our invitation to brokenness and surrender, an opportunity to dive deeper into submission to the Lord. What we don't seem to realize is that those waves will continue to pound away until we decide to trust Him and obey Him.

In Scripture, we find an incredible twist on our typical view of struggle and strife. The author of the book of Hebrews says it bluntly: "Endure hardship as discipline" (Heb. 12:7). What is striking, however, is that the author expects us to be encouraged by the Lord's discipline. In fact, the author shows that it is one of the best things that can happen to us.

Let's put the Hebrews passage into context. The letter was written to Jewish converts to Christianity who may have been tempted to return to their Judaic roots. They suffered persecution, lost property, and were—like so many of us—growing weary of the battle.

> You have forgotten that word of encouragement
> that addresses you as sons:

"My son, do not make light of the Lord's discipline,
        and do not lose heart when he rebukes you,
because the Lord disciplines those he loves,
        and he punishes everyone he accepts as a son."

Endure hardship as a discipline; God is treating you
as sons. For what son is not disciplined by his father?
If you are not disciplined (and everyone undergoes
discipline), then you are illegitimate children and
not true sons. Moreover, we have all had human
fathers who disciplined us and we respected them
for it. How much more should we submit to the
Father of our spirits and live! Our fathers disciplined us for a little while as they thought best; but
God disciplines us for our good, that we may share
in his holiness. No discipline seems pleasant at the
time, but painful. Later on, however, it produces a
harvest of righteousness and peace for those who
have been trained by it.

Therefore, strengthen your feeble arms and
weak knees. "Make level paths for your feet," so that
the lame may not be disabled, but rather healed.
(Heb. 12:5–13)

The idea of discipline as encouragement ("encouragement" in
this passage, from the Greek word *paraclesis,* is less about comfort
and more along the lines of a forceful exhortation) is counterintui-
tive. Most of us don't wish for a time-out or a spanking when we're

young or for a speeding ticket from a police officer when we're older. We experience discipline as a nuisance—*or worse.*

Yet the meaning behind this Scripture passage definitely speaks to me. God is our heavenly Father, and part of a father's role is to provide discipline for his children. If we stop to think about it, an earthly father wouldn't take the time to correctly discipline a son or daughter unless he loved his child. It is the same with our spiritual Father. Hardship is a sign of His discipline, and His discipline is evidence of His love. It's one way He says, "You are *My* child. I care about you, and I'm going to do what it takes to strengthen you and prepare you for a better life ahead."

My parents divorced when I was young. For most of the following years, I didn't see much of my dad. I understood that he had a problem with alcohol and that many times he'd let down my mom, my brothers and sisters, and me. But he was still my dad, and I loved him. I yearned for him to play sports with me and take me hunting and fishing. I wanted him to teach me how to pound crooked nails into scraps of wood, build a rocket ship to the moon, and design the best go-cart on this side of the planet. I wanted to know that he loved me back and believed in me.

And so, strange as it may sound, I would have welcomed his discipline, too. Not anything abusive, of course. But if I'd been harassing my siblings or skipping school or stealing candy from the corner store, and my dad had to step in and do what was necessary— a time-out, a grounding, a spanking? You bet! I might not have enjoyed it much at the time, but I think deep down I would have understood and realized it was right and good. In a way, I would have found it comforting. It would have been visible evidence that my dad was involved in my life, that he cared enough to go through the not-so-pleasant process of teaching me the consequences of my actions or inactions.

Today, I realize I would have given just about anything to experience this kind of discipline from my dad when I was growing up. That opportunity is gone, yet now I have another Father who continues to actively work in my life and discipline me. And just as the Scripture says, that is a source of great encouragement to me. It means that my heavenly Father loves me.

After reading this, you might be thinking, *Is this guy saying that every time something bad happens in my life, God is punishing me?* Again, I'm not a Bible scholar, but I don't think that's the point of this passage. I don't believe that the Lord orchestrates every trial we encounter. Some He does; others He allows. Some are simply the result of evil in the world. Yet we are told to view *all* our troubles as discipline. It's not because God is a stern taskmaster who wants to see us suffer (although He is capable of that). It's because we should be encouraged by His discipline. It's because He uses all of our trials for good, for His glory, and to invite us to draw nearer to Him and to submit to His better plan for our lives.

That's not punishment. *That's love.*

Promises

There is even more for us to be encouraged about in this amazing passage of Scripture. We can find a number of promises embedded within its words.

Look again at Hebrews 12:11: "No discipline seems pleasant at the time, but painful. Later on, however, it produces a harvest of righteousness and peace for those who have been trained by it." In other words, if we allow the lesson of God's discipline to sink in—if we discover and accept His purpose in our troubles—we will eventually gain righteousness and peace. What does it mean to be righteous? To act in accord with God's law, free from guilt and sin. What does it mean to have the kind of peace offered here? To understand that no trial is too devastating or overwhelming for Him, that we can confidently face *anything* when we are walking with and depending on the Lord.

Now take another look at verses 12 and 13: "Therefore, strengthen your feeble arms and weak knees. 'Make level paths for your feet,' so that the lame may not be disabled, but rather healed."

What do these words imply? They are consistent with what we've said before: *The choice is ours. We* can decide to strengthen arms and knees and feet, to forge a level path. We are not at the mercy of our troubles *if* we accept both the discipline and the One who disciplines. The promise here is not that all troubles will be waved away, but that we will experience healing. I don't know about you, but I find that's something to be excited about.

We can boil it all down to this: *Surrender leads to strength*.

If you're still fighting that war, I urge you to lay down your sword right now. Record on paper your willingness to submit to the Lord, and ask for no terms. Just sign your name. Allow yourself to be broken. Give up and give all of yourself to Him.

You won't regret it.

Chapter 5

God's Invitation

When I was growing up, if you had said that one day I'd be president of a large organization such as Focus on the Family, I'm sure no one in my family would have believed it. My siblings might have believed I'd eventually pursue a career in acting, though. They knew firsthand that, like many last-born children, I had a flair for the dramatic.

I remember well a day when I demonstrated my drama skills. I was seven years old, living in a small house in Yucca Valley on the edge of California's Mojave Desert. I was bored and lonely and wanted someone to play with. My dad was out of the picture, and my mom was at work. My four older brothers and sisters—Mike, Dave, Dee Dee, and Kim—were home but busy with their own activities. They weren't in the mood to entertain a pesky younger brother. So I moped around the house, mumbling loud enough for them to hear, "Nobody cares about me. Nobody loves me." It had no effect. In fact, they taunted me for my remarks.

I decided it was time to up the stakes. I pulled a steak knife out of a kitchen drawer, walked up to Mike while holding the knife pointed at my stomach, and said in my most theatric voice, "Go ahead, just shove it in. I know that's what you want. I know you want to get rid of me!"

Mike didn't even look up from what he was doing. He knew that it was a put-on and that I was only trying to get attention.

I didn't let Mike's stoicism stop me, of course. I tried the same ploy on each of my other siblings. Sadly, the result was the same.

Did I give up at this point and go read a comic book? Not a chance! I grabbed a white-and-green striped shoebox, packed it with the essential ingredients for any seven-year-old ready to leave his ungrateful family and strike out on his own—a rust-colored sweater, four tomatoes, a salt shaker, and the aforementioned steak knife— and walked out the front door, slamming it as I left.

Now what? I wondered.

I found myself moving in the direction of Calhan's Restaurant, where my mom managed and worked as a waitress. A mile and many footsteps later, feeling more sorry for myself than ever, I walked in, found my mother (who was busy serving a customer), and said in a pathetic tone, "Mom, nobody loves me."

Mom couldn't really deal with her forlorn son at that moment, of course. She told me to go sit in her car. So I did. Then I got hungry, so I cut up my tomatoes and ate them (properly salted, just the way I liked them). The tomatoes made me feel a little better, and a little tired. I put on the sweater, laid down, and soon was asleep. The next thing I knew, Mom was tucking me into my bed back home. I decided I'd stick with my family for a while longer.

My point is not that I missed my calling as the next Tom Hanks. My point here is that we all want to be loved, we hate to be ignored, and sometimes we'll do almost anything to get the people we care about to notice us.

I think God can be like that too.

We know from the first commandment that we are to have no other gods before the Lord (Ex. 20:3). We know from the second commandment that we are not to worship anyone or anything other than our Lord; He is a jealous God (Ex. 20:4–5). He loves us. He desires our praise and worship and prayers and attention.

The Lord seeks a personal, intimate relationship with each of His children—with me and with you. And when nothing else works, He sometimes allows life to take a turn for the dramatic in order for us to regain our focus. I can't emphasize enough that your illness, your job loss, and your ongoing problems with your son or daughter may be more than unfortunate. And I'm certain that these problems are not a sign that God is out to "get you."

I believe that what's often going on is that the Lord is waving His hand in front of your face. He's saying, "Remember Me? I created you. I died for you. I love you! Won't you talk to Me—not for two minutes as you drive to work, not with a superficial 'please bless my day tomorrow, God' before you fall asleep, but from your heart, sharing your innermost dreams and fears and joys? I want to be close to you—closer than anyone."

When you think about it, it's pretty incredible that the Creator of the universe is this concerned about wanting one-on-one time with each of us. We should be grateful and in awe—even when His methods aren't what we might choose.

Is God *always* the source of our troubles, the One who enables our trials to occur? No, I don't think so. But I believe it's more common than we realize. So often, our hard times result in the Lord inviting us into deeper intimacy with Him. When we accept that invitation, it brings Him joy. But the benefit of deeper intimacy with God is far greater to us than to Him. We get to enter into the most important relationship of our lives, one that transforms our existence. Through this relationship, we will discover the source of peace, joy, goodness, and strength.

I would rather go through a lifetime of trials *with* God than a lifetime of ease without Him. If you asked a man named Charlie Wedemeyer what he prefers, I think he'd say the same thing.

A Roller-Coaster Ride

Charlie Wedemeyer was thirty years old on the day he noticed a weakness in his hands. A math teacher at Los Gatos High School in California, he was writing a problem on the classroom chalkboard when he realized he had to grip his chalk tighter than usual to finish.

It was a strange feeling for someone so physically gifted. As a high school athlete in Hawaii, he'd been named the state's "prep player of the decade." He later played football at Michigan State University and was chosen for two college all-star teams. He'd turned that experience into success as a teacher and football coach at Los Gatos.

Charlie figured his hand trouble probably stemmed from old football injuries and dismissed it. But as the weeks passed, the weakness grew worse. He found it difficult to shave in the morning. He had trouble working the keys to unlock his car. Finally,

Charlie submitted to a series of medical tests. The resulting diagnosis was unimaginable—Charlie had amyotrophic lateral sclerosis (ALS), the degenerative and terminal condition known as "Lou Gehrig's disease." The doctor estimated Charlie had less than a year to live.

Charlie couldn't believe it. *I don't feel sick. I'm certainly not sick enough to die. It can't be true.* On the drive home from the doctor's office, the news began to sink in. He thought about his wife, Lucy, and children, Carri and Kale. *If that's true, I won't ever be able to see my children grow up!* He ran a red light before realizing he had to pull over and get control of his emotions. Tears were rolling down his face. It was the beginning of a roller-coaster ride.

As Charlie's condition worsened, the Wedemeyers tried a host of alternative treatments, from acupuncture to consulting a Hawaiian healer. Some helped him feel better, but none were effective in slowing the progress of the disease. Eventually, Charlie could no longer use his arms at all. His legs betrayed him too; he was humiliated by several bad falls in public and began using a wheelchair. He had trouble eating and lost an alarming amount of weight. The cost of treatments, equipment, doctor exams, and at-home nursing care drained the Wedemeyers' financial resources.

Charlie fought on. He had a tremendous will to live and received amazing support from Lucy and the rest of his family and friends. As the years passed, Charlie far exceeded the early predictions of his demise. Yet the struggle seemed only to get harder. He had terrible coughing fits. He couldn't sleep. At one point, feeling frustrated and defeated, Charlie told Lucy that she and the children would be better off if he died.

By January 1985, more than eight years after Charlie's first symptoms appeared, he weighed just 115 pounds, and every breath was a
battle. One difficult night, as Lucy, the children, and a nurse all tried
to help, Charlie stopped breathing entirely. His son, Kale, jammed
the catheter end of a suction machine hose into Charlie's throat to
clear away congestion and open an airway. His daughter, Carri, ran
to call 911. When paramedics arrived, Charlie was breathing again,
but gasping. He stabilized after the paramedics administered oxygen.

Though her husband made it through the night, Lucy realized
they had reached a new low. She called Charlie's family in Hawaii
and urged them to come a few days early for a fund-raising banquet
to be held in his honor. She wasn't sure he would live to see the event.

Charlie Wedemeyer's body was broken. Despite his zest for life
and love for his family, his spirit was breaking. He wanted to keep on
living. He just didn't see how his body would allow that to happen.

He had to admit that the future was out of his hands.

An Undeniable Presence

One late afternoon just four days before the banquet, Lucy left home
for a meeting. Ramona, a new nurse, was just starting her shift and
another nurse, Leslyn, was about to go home. It had been a particularly difficult day. Every time Lucy or Leslyn had tried to feed Charlie
a little soup, he'd gagged, triggering a frightening coughing fit. Now
Charlie was tired, but he didn't want to fall asleep. He was afraid if
he did, he might choke to death.

"You're having a terrible time getting air today, aren't you?" said
Ramona. She asked if she could pray for Charlie. She and Charlie
had talked about God before. They both believed in Him, though

Ramona seemed to have a more intimate faith and relationship with the Lord.

Charlie agreed to Ramona's request, but he was a little startled when she placed her hands on his chest and began praying aloud, "Dear Lord, I just ask that You will help Charlie breathe easier so he can sleep. And clear his throat so he can swallow and eat something. Please comfort Charlie and bring peace to his heart."

Charlie remembers the moment well. As he watched Ramona pray, he felt something begin to happen:

> I felt a combination of power and peace I'd never known … cours[ing] from my chest out to my arms and legs, through my entire being.… [I]t filled the room, a tidal wave of calm and comfort washing over me, a loving presence that held and surrounded me.…
>
> I realized I too was weeping.… The emotion was just so intense, so tangible, so overpoweringly peaceful that it filled me to overflowing and the tears just poured out.
>
> Leslyn … too was crying. Later, she told me that as Ramona prayed, she'd felt such a presence in the room that she kept looking around to see who had come in.
>
> We all knew who it was. I certainly had no question. God was suddenly real to me in a way I'd never imagined before. I felt His love and care for me. I knew He was real because I felt His undeniable presence and power in me and around me.[1]

Charlie felt shock when he looked at the shriveled amaryllis plant at the foot of his bed. A friend had left it a few days before. Lucy had watered it and applied plant food, hoping to get it to bloom, but nothing had worked. Charlie had asked a nurse to throw it away, but she'd forgotten. Only a few minutes before, Charlie remembered, its three buds had remained tightly closed. Now, impossibly, they were in full bloom.

Leslyn, crying, called Lucy and asked her to come home. When Lucy arrived, they all tried to explain what had happened. Then Ramona said, "You know, God wants us to be able to know His presence and help in our lives every day. We can all have that relationship with Him if we want it."[2]

Soon she was leading Charlie and Lucy to ask for the Lord's forgiveness and invite Jesus into their lives. That night, Charlie enjoyed his best sleep in months.

However we choose to interpret this experience, it changed Charlie's life. From that point on, he felt a new excitement about his faith in God. Though he'd gone to church all his life, he now realized that the Lord wanted something more from him—*a personal relationship*. A few weeks after Ramona's prayers, an old friend named Maria came to visit Charlie and Lucy. She explained that praying and reading the Bible regularly were essential for strengthening a relationship with the Lord.

Maria began to visit Charlie regularly. During her visits, she and Charlie talked and prayed and read from God's Word nearly nonstop until evening. When it was late, Maria would announce that she needed to get to bed. Charlie always said something like, "How about another minute?" or "Just one more verse before we quit?"

He soaked up the Bible like a sponge. So much of what Charlie learned made sense like never before. Charlie found that because of his brokenness, God became both real and relational in a way he'd never imagined.

David, writing in Psalm 34:18, says, "The LORD is close to the brokenhearted and saves those who are crushed in spirit." God is always with us, so what exactly does it mean that He is close to the brokenhearted? I believe that when we are broken we are better able to sense His nearness and are more open to allowing Him deep into our hearts.

David goes on to say, "A righteous man may have many troubles, but the LORD delivers him from them all; he protects all his bones, not one of them will be broken" (vv. 19–20). How literally, you might ask, should we take this passage? Does it promise the "good life" to all who are righteous? Does it mean that if we pray for relief from our trials and God doesn't seem to answer that we aren't righteous?

I don't think that's the case at all. There are plenty of examples of righteous men—the apostle Paul is certainly one—who struggled on with a "thorn in [the] flesh" even after praying for deliverance (2 Cor. 12:7). So what, you might ask, are we to make of the words of Scripture here?

I think David is talking about a different kind of deliverance. It could be in the form of physical relief, but he's probably talking primarily about the spiritual. When he says that the Lord protects "all his bones," he's talking about a person's whole being—including his eternal soul. The message I see over and over in Scripture is that God is most concerned about the condition of our eternal spirits, not our temporary bodies.

I don't claim to have special insight into the purposes of God, but it appears to me that when Charlie Wedemeyer contracted ALS, the Lord used it to draw him and others closer to Himself. He never healed Charlie. Yet by His grace, Charlie has lived with his disease for more than three decades. He and Lucy have made countless speaking appearances, with Lucy translating Charlie's nearly inaudible whispers for audiences around the world. Their story has been told in movies and books and inspired people of every age.

Charlie says that "God gives us a choice when we face difficult circumstances."[3] We can choose misery or "we can choose to face our trials with God's help, knowing that we'll come out the other side as stronger people for the experience."[4] That doesn't necessarily mean that our trials will end. But whatever happens we, like Charlie, will gain a new strength for dealing with them. We can discover meaning in our circumstances and a purpose that helps others overcome their own pain.

The choice is ours.

When God Is Hidden

God is pursuing us. Jesus said, "Here I am! I stand at the door and knock. If anyone hears my voice and opens the door, I will come in and eat with him, and he with me" (Rev. 3:20). At the center of our being, a relationship with the Lord—deep, personal, abiding, satisfying, soul-filling—is what we all want and need more than anything else. Many of us don't even realize it, but it is the hole in our hearts that yearns to be filled. We want to *know* Him. We desire to be in His presence.

Even though my family rarely went to church and I really had no idea what God was about, as a child I still had a sense of His presence and purpose for me. I remember a time when I was five years old, walking down the street with my dad. It was a sunny day, and I was wearing shorts. Now, I need to let you know that I have a ton of freckles on the backs of my legs. On that day when I was five, Dad suddenly looked down and said, "Man, where'd you get all those freckles on your legs?"

I didn't even think about my answer, yet it was completely sincere. I looked up at my dad and said, "I guess that's just how God made me."

My dad laughed. What I recall most vividly, though, is the feeling I had at that moment. I meant what I'd said. I knew the Lord was with me and that He'd made me, *freckles and all*. I didn't know how I knew it. I just *knew*.

Followers of Christ come to this realization sooner or later. It's part of what compels us to reach for Jesus. One way or another, we encounter Him and come to understand that we're not an accident. We see that He created us for a purpose and that a huge part of that purpose is to be in a relationship with Him.

Recently, recording artist Danny Oertli sang during our chapel time at Focus. While introducing his song "I Thought You Should Know," Danny told us how he prayed for his children every night. One evening he was praying for his adopted son, Jack, and his prayer went something like this: "Lord, put a bubble around him and let nothing ever happen to this kid. Keep him safe emotionally and physically and spiritually." I've certainly offered many similar prayers for my two sons.

That night, though, Danny had the sudden sensation that God was in the room, almost as if Jesus were tapping him on the shoulder. It prompted him to think about his life and how the most sacred times he'd had with the Lord had come during periods of struggle and pain, times when he had nowhere else to turn but to God.

At that moment, it all made sense. Danny realized that he didn't want Jack to be safe. He wanted Jack to love Jesus. To me, this is more evidence that our journey isn't about living a long and safe life. It *is* truly about our relationship with the Lord.

When tragedy strikes or tough times threaten to overwhelm us, we might be tempted to get angry with God. Our relationship grows strained. We may turn away from God and look for ways to deaden our pain—through alcohol, drugs, food, sex, or even sleep. But in the long run, none of these things help at all. They only add to the distance between the Lord and us. We achieve genuine relief only when we turn to Him.

Some of us find ourselves in a different place, however. We're hurting and we know that we need the Lord. We pray and seek Him. Yet He seems absent. We aren't hearing His voice. We don't sense His presence. We feel abandoned. And so, once again, the temptation is to do whatever it takes to remove the pain.

What Is That All About?

I don't pretend to have all the answers, but I will make some observations. I think in this case, it's a little like being a child in your bedroom at night. It's dark, and so black that you can't see anything. Your door is closed, so you can't hear anything outside your room. Yet your favorite pillow and nightstand are still there. Your parents are nearby too. They haven't left you. In fact, your mother is in the kitchen preparing lunch for the next day. She's humming as she works, because she's baking chocolate chip cookies to surprise you.

It's a simple illustration, but you get the idea—circumstances may make it hard for us to sense God's presence, yet He's still there. He hasn't left us. And more often than we realize, His "hiddenness" allows Him to work on our behalf in a way that wouldn't be possible if we could see Him.

To take the analogy further, if you're a child in bed at night, you could jump out of bed, turn on the light, and rush into the kitchen to make sure Mom is still around. You could do that all night long. But that isn't what's best for you, is it? It would leave you exhausted the next day, and it would spoil the surprise of the chocolate chip cookies. You'd be far better off to trust that Mom is there, that she has things under control, and that all you need to do now is go to sleep.

Author, counselor, and psychologist Larry Crabb describes it this way:

> [God] vanishes from our sight to do what He could not do if we could see Him. In the spiritual journey, I know of nothing so difficult to believe. But it's true.
>
> Think of those three hours of darkness on the cross. Jesus screamed in agony, "God, where are You?" God said nothing. But it was during that exact time that God was in the Son reconciling the world to Himself.

Imagine the comfort we would experience and
the hope we would feel if we realized that during
His felt absence, Jesus is working to cut the chain
from our ankles, to remove the weight that keeps us
from flying.[5]

According to Larry Crabb, the Lord does some of His best work
in us when He seems most absent from us. I like that. It means that
when we are in despair and don't sense the presence of God, He is
more attuned to us than ever, even if we can't see it or understand it.
It means that He uses that despair—if we allow Him to use it—to
prepare us for a new and deeper version of His love.

If anyone throughout biblical history came to understand this
concept, it was Job. Here was a man who had everything: ten children,
seven thousand sheep, three thousand camels, five hundred yoke of
oxen, five hundred donkeys, and many servants. More important, in
the Lord's eyes, he was "blameless and upright; he feared God and
shunned evil" (Job 1:1). Yet when Satan challenged Job's righteousness, God allowed Job to lose *everything*.

How did Job respond? The tragedy was real. He immediately
went into mourning and must have felt unbelievable pain. Yet he did
not reject God, instead he said: "The LORD gave and the LORD has
taken away; may the name of the LORD be praised" (1:21).

Later, after becoming afflicted with painful sores and after his
wife urged him to curse God, Job wished for death. But even here
he did not turn away from the Lord. Instead, he said, "What I
feared has come upon me; what I dreaded has happened to me"
(3:25).

Some will read this verse and say that Job feared the loss of his family and possessions. But I believe his heart was so in sync with the Lord's that his greatest fear was separation from his heavenly Father. Was he mourning the deaths of his children, his health, and his wealth? Yes! But even greater than these losses was the pain of feeling removed from God's approval and affection. Job despaired over what seemed the end of his relationship with the Lord.

It wasn't the end of Job's relationship with God, of course. God recognized Job's steadfast faith and blessed the second half of Job's life even more than the first, giving him ten more children, twice as much livestock, and allowing him to live 140 years.

Did Job's relationship with the Lord grow deeper after his time of turmoil? Did he emerge from the experience with a strengthened faith? Is he enjoying eternity in heaven right now? We can't answer those questions, but we can make an educated guess. I'm looking forward to one day finding out.

Desperate Love

When I held a steak knife in the air all those years ago and threatened to impale myself in front of my brothers and sisters, it was an immature attempt at meeting a genuine need. I felt lonely that day. Empty. I wanted to be loved. So I pretended to resort to the most desperate of measures to obtain that love.

There is a kind of desperate love that has nothing to do with pretending. Patrick Morley once wrote a story about a father and son—Phil and Mark Littleford—who flew by seaplane to a secluded Alaskan bay for a day of fishing with two other men. The next morning, when the group tried to take off, the plane managed only a low, circular pattern. They realized one of the pontoons had been punctured and was filled with water. It was dragging the plane down.

The plane crashed into the water and capsized. Everyone was alive, but they couldn't find any safety equipment. After a prayer, the three men and twelve-year-old Mark jumped into the bay to swim to shore. The water was icy cold, and the riptide strong. Two of the men finally reached the Alaskan shore, exhausted. When they looked back, they saw Phil and Mark on the horizon, arm in arm; they were being swept out to sea. The men knew Phil could have made it to shore and surmised that Mark wasn't a strong enough swimmer. Phil wasn't going to leave his son behind. Phil chose to die with his boy rather than live without him.[6]

The Lord's love for you is like this. It's so desperate that He is willing to let you suffer—though it brings Him no pleasure—so that you have a chance at the glory of an eternal relationship with Him. He would even die to make this possible. In fact, that's exactly what He did on the cross.

God may be stirring up trouble in your life or allowing trials to occur in order to draw you nearer to Him. He won't make you come to Him. This is His way of inviting you into His arms.

The next move is up to you.

Chapter 6

Acceptance and Trust

The apostle Paul once made a remarkable statement to the members of the early church at Philippi, the Roman colony in Macedonia. He wrote, "I have learned to be content whatever the circumstances. I know what it is to be in need, and I know what it is to have plenty. I have learned the secret of being content in any and every situation, whether well fed or hungry, whether living in plenty or in want. I can do everything through him who gives me strength" (Phil. 4:11–13).

I don't know about you, but when someone announces that they have a secret, I'm curious to know what it is. And when that secret offers as much as Paul's does, I am especially curious!

This passage, in fact, is one of the most important in Scripture for exploring the concept of strength. It contains one of the biggest promises in the Bible. If we can discover how to be truly content "in any and every situation," we will know a peace that few people ever achieve. That is a rare and invaluable strength.

Generally speaking, the words *content* and *at peace* are rarely used to describe the human species. Our attitude is better depicted by the complaint of that comic-strip icon of wisdom, six-year-old Calvin of *Calvin and Hobbes*: "My life could be a lot better than it is. I'm happy, but it's not like I'm ecstatic."[1]

We seem to always hope, and often expect, our lot to improve.

Sooner or later, however, we are confronted with a circumstance that rocks our world. For Calvin, it's a babysitter named Rosalyn. For those of us in real life, it's the death of a parent or spouse or child, divorce, infertility, cancer, a heart attack, sexual abuse, loss of a job, a car accident, a repossessed home, or any of a thousand other tragedies or trials. And when it happens, many of us, especially those of us who are Christians, wonder: "God, how could You let this happen?"

In these moments we desperately need to know Paul's secret.

Moving Day

On May 27, 2008, Leslie McGill was driving her Chevrolet SUV on Highway 20 in Madison Parish, Louisiana. Beside her in the passenger seat sat her daughter, thirteen-year-old Marissa. Riding in the back seat was her son, eight-year-old Gabriel—along with two dogs and an assortment of items that filled the car to overflowing.

It was moving day for the McGill family. Leslie's husband, Ken, had taken a job in Dallas a couple of months earlier. Leslie had sold their former home in Hattiesburg, Mississippi, and was looking forward to uniting their family. They didn't even have a home in Texas yet, but it didn't matter because they would be together again.

Starting over in a new state would be a big change, but Leslie was determined to view the move as an opportunity and an adventure. She and Marissa were already talking about taking their dogs for walks together and training them to be "civilized." Although Leslie felt exhaustion from all the last-minute preparations, the weather was beautiful, and they were on their way. It seemed their adventure was off to a great start.

When the McGills passed through Vicksburg and crossed a river, Leslie pointed out the sign that said they were entering Louisiana. It was time for one of their silly family traditions. "Good-bye, Mississippi!" she, Marissa, and Gabriel called out in unison.

Leslie smiled. It still amazed her that she had been blessed with these two wonderful children. Every mother believes her children are special, of course. But in Marissa's case, others were noticing too. She had a unique quality that attracted people. Some friends of the McGills seemed to visit as much to see Marissa as her parents. She was bright, always smiling, and greatly concerned for others. She loved playing with her little brother and going to his baseball games. As a seventh grader, she'd made the varsity soccer team. For her performance on academic test scores, she'd earned a Grand Recognition award from Duke University. She was already talking about attending Duke when it was time for college.

What amazed Leslie, however, was the depth of Marissa's faith in and relationship with the Lord. After she met people, Marissa would wonder if they were saved and ask permission to invite them to church. She knew her Bible forward and backward. She wrote a devotional for the members of her team. Though Leslie didn't know it then, Marissa had recorded in her journal that it was okay if she never had a boyfriend, because Jesus was all she needed. Marissa's dream was to grow up and become a missionary in Africa.

Leslie wasn't sure her own relationship with the Lord was as strong as her daughter's relationship. Leslie had first made a commitment to the Lord at the age of eleven. She'd always considered herself an "okay" Christian and had become more intentional about her faith and example since having children. Yet she wanted more. In January, Leslie and Marissa had joined in a church fast. Leslie's goal for the fast was for God to deepen her faith. She didn't realize just how soon that opportunity would come.

Around noon on the drive to Texas, the McGills stopped briefly to pick up fast food and chicken sandwiches. To stay on schedule, they decided to eat on the way. As they moved past the small town of Mound, however, one of the dogs—Lulu, a chocolate lab puppy—started a commotion by getting into the lunch in Gabriel's lap. Marissa turned around to help, holding Gabriel's french fries and trying to keep Lulu away with her other hand. There was no other traffic, so Leslie decided to also reach one hand back to help pull Lulu away from her son.

Leslie's eyes were diverted from the road for only a few moments, but it was long enough for the vehicle to silently veer to the right. The SUV was on cruise control and the road had no rumble strip to warn her. When Leslie looked back, the Chevrolet was slipping past the shoulder. Leslie quickly turned left. The car began fishtailing, and the kids began yelling.

Oh my gosh, Leslie thought. *This is really bad.*

Leslie couldn't regain control. The SUV plunged down an embankment and into a large tree, bounced back up the embankment, then rolled over and down until the same tree, now uprooted, broke in half and fell on the vehicle.

Leslie realized she was hanging from her seat belt above Marissa, the Chevrolet tilted at a crazy angle. Gabriel was yelling and crying, but Marissa was silent and unmoving. Leslie and Gabriel scrambled out of the blown-out sunroof and went to Marissa. When Leslie touched her arm, she sensed that her daughter was already gone. Leslie felt for a pulse; there was none.

Up on the road, a car stopped. People hurried down, then led Leslie and Gabriel away from the wreck, insisting that they sit on a log. "Please get my daughter," Leslie said. "Please save her."

"We'll get to her," someone said.

Leslie sat next to Gabriel, who was still crying. She couldn't believe this was happening. It had to be a bad dream.

Suddenly Gabriel stopped crying, looked up at his mother, and spoke in a voice of complete calm: "Mom. Mom. It's okay. If she's dead, it's all part of God's plan." Then he started crying again.

But for Leslie, at that moment, it wasn't okay. She and Gabriel were taken to a hospital. Leslie kept her eyes shut tight; she couldn't face what was happening. Finally, an hour and a half after the accident, a coroner told her what she already knew in her heart: *Marissa was gone.*

Suddenly, everything in Leslie's life flipped upside down. Her beloved daughter was dead. As the shock wore off in the days that followed, she was overwhelmed by grief and guilt and filled with questions.

God, I don't understand this. How could You let this happen? Why? Are You punishing me? Did I love Marissa too much, so You had to take her away? How can I continue to love You when it feels like in a single moment You've completely messed up my life?

Leslie felt hurt and confused, and now she had an incredibly important decision to make. It was as if she were standing at a precipice, looking out over a frightening drop into a beautiful blue sea. After what had happened to her only daughter, would she still trust the Lord with her life and dive in? Or would she turn away?[2]

Paul's Secret

As any of us would after a time of personal tragedy, Leslie McGill was desperately trying to understand the mysterious methods of God. Even if we accept the idea that the freedom the Lord gives us also allows evil in the world and enables us to make choices that can lead to heartache, and even if we acknowledge that trials sometimes have a holy purpose, we still can't help wondering why God would allow the death of someone like Marissa. She seemed to have an incredible future ahead of her, she loved and wanted to serve Jesus, and she might have been an example of faith to hundreds, thousands, or even millions. It doesn't make sense.

As much as we want to know the answer to the question "Why, God?" we may not find it during our earthly lifetime. Scripture clearly points out that we will not know the Lord's ways fully until we see Him:

- "For my thoughts are not your thoughts, neither are your ways my ways," declares the LORD. "As the heavens are higher than the earth, so are my ways higher than your ways and my thoughts than your thoughts." (Isa. 55:8–9)

- The secret things belong to the LORD our God. (Deut. 29:29)
- It is the glory of God to conceal a matter. (Prov. 25:2)
- As you do not know the path of the wind, or how the body is formed in a mother's womb, so you cannot understand the work of God, the Maker of all things. (Eccl. 11:5)
- Now, we see but a poor reflection as in a mirror; then we shall see face to face. Now I know in part; then I shall know fully, even as I am fully known. (1 Cor. 13:12)

You may wonder, then, if God isn't going to explain Himself, where does that leave us? I think we're all at that precipice with Leslie, confronting a vital decision. We might think of it like this: Will we allow our circumstances to define God, or will we choose to let God define our circumstances?

You may have noticed a pattern in this book. We've seen that whenever troubles arrive at our doorstep, we're presented with a series of choices. We start at the crossroads and see three paths: *beaten, bitter,* or *broken.* Do we surrender to God's will or chart our own course? Do we withdraw into ourselves or accept the Lord's invitation to move into a deeper relationship with Him— "If anyone hears my voice and opens the door, I will come in" (Rev. 3:20)?

When trouble arrives and we don't understand why, there is yet another decision we must make. If we know Paul's secret, we can be confident of making the right choice. I believe the secret is simply this: *Accept what's happened even if it doesn't make sense, and trust that God is in control.*

No Middle Ground

Most any counselor will tell you that it's wise to accept what you cannot change. To resist against that which is immovable or inevitable is frustrating at the least and harmful if taken to extremes. We delude ourselves if we ignore or deny what is in front of us.

What we are talking about here goes beyond good mental health, however. We must accept not only what is happening in our lives but also the fact that God has everything under control and that He is using it for our ultimate benefit. When we accept this truth, we significantly strengthen our relationship with the Lord and our faith. If we reject this truth, we can slide toward despair and death, because trying to make sense of trial and tragedy without God does not work. This is the point that leads to so much pain, confusion, and depression. It is one of the factors that makes some people grow depressed and suicidal.

What is both wonderful and frightening about this dilemma is that God does not allow us to remain undecided. There is no middle ground.

You may remember Jesus' statement:

> "I know your deeds, that you are neither cold nor hot. I wish you were either one or the other! So, because you are lukewarm—neither hot nor cold— I am about to spit you out of my mouth. You say, 'I am rich; I have acquired wealth and do not need a thing.' But you do not realize that you are wretched, pitiful, poor, blind and naked. I counsel you to buy from me gold refined in the fire, so you can become

> rich; and white clothes to wear, so you can cover your shameful nakedness; and salve to put on your eyes, so you can see." (Rev. 3:15–18)

The Lord is so offended by our attempts to put off this vital choice—to move toward Him or away from Him—that He compares it to vomiting. He insists that we trust and depend on Him or simply reject Him. He asks us to choose either salvation or despair, life or death. And if we seek to avoid the decision, I believe the Lord confronts us with more and more tribulations until we take a stand.

Perhaps these troubles come in the form of silly mundane things that can irritate us—the grocery store that's out of flour when we need it, the earring that disappears, the driver who cuts us off on the freeway. Sometimes these troubles can be heartwrenching, life-altering events like the death of a loved one. Each instance, I believe, is an opportunity. On a daily basis, we either accept and trust or turn away. We're always moving in one direction or the other—toward eternal love and strength or toward devastation.

It Is Well with My Soul

Jennifer Rothschild was a typical kid at Miami's Glades Junior High School when she noticed she seemed to have more trouble negotiating dark stairwells or catching a ball than her classmates. It made her feel awkward and self-conscious. Finally, she told her mother about her struggles.

A visit to an ophthalmologist led to a stronger glasses prescription, yet the problem soon grew worse. This time, Jennifer visited an eye hospital for a series of tests. She and her parents met with the doctors to hear the results. To their dismay, they learned that Jennifer had retinitis pigmentosa, a degenerative disease that slowly eats away the retina of the eye. There was no way to correct the damage and no cure. At age fifteen, Jennifer was already legally blind. The disease would continue to progress until she lived in complete darkness.

On the drive home from the hospital that day, Jennifer's father tightly gripped the steering wheel. Her mother sat next to him in the front passenger seat. Jennifer sat alone in the back. Everyone was silent, still trying to process the devastating news.

Jennifer's mind raced with questions: *How will I finish high school? Will I ever go to college? How will I know what I look like? Will I ever get a date or a boyfriend? Will I ever get married?* Then she realized that she would never have the chance to drive a car. She'd been looking forward to having "wheels" for a long time. Now, suddenly, that dream evaporated.

Forty-five minutes later, they arrived home. Jennifer went straight to the living room and sat down at the family piano and began to play. She'd taken lessons off and on for eight years, though she hadn't always been an enthusiastic student. Now, the familiar feel and sounds of the old piano comforted her.

Jennifer didn't attempt one of the few songs she'd memorized. Instead, she played a melody by ear, one she knew well but had never tried on the piano. The song was "It Is Well with My Soul."

"Some people have told me it was a miracle that I could sit down at the piano that day and begin to play by ear for the first time," Jennifer remembers. "Perhaps it was. Who knows? But to me, there was a bigger miracle that dark day.

"The miracle was not that I played 'It Is Well with My Soul,' but that it actually *was* well with my soul. Now, more than twenty years later, I look back and wonder at all that has happened. I still can't see, of course, and I know well the hardships that blindness brings. Yet I have been blessed with a wonderful husband and two sons, as well as a meaningful speaking ministry. God has been good to me.

"On that day so long ago—in the hospital, on the ride home, and at the piano—even as I mourned my loss, I looked into the heart of my Teacher. I knew His Word and His character, and they were what allowed me to say then—and still say today—*whatever my lot ... it is well with my soul.*"[3]

At the age of fifteen, Jennifer Rothschild stood at the precipice. Facing the crushing prospect of a lifetime of blindness, she had to decide if she would accept it and dive even deeper into trusting the Lord, or if she would resist a God who allows such misfortune and enter a world of anger, bitterness, and despair. Jennifer chose acceptance and trust.

It's a choice that's easy to see on paper but difficult to implement when the life that's been turned upside down is our own. It can be harder still if we are trying to hold on to a pair of common expectations that may prevent us from making the choice God desires.

Two Kingdoms in Conflict

When disciples of John the Baptist asked Jesus why His disciples did not fast as they did, Jesus answered by pointing out that no one would pour new wine into old wineskins. At the time, goatskins were used to hold wine. A used skin, already stretched, would break, spilling the wine. A new skin, on the other hand, would stretch as the grape juice fermented and expanded, preserving the wine (Matt. 9:14–17).

What Jesus meant is that in the presence of the Son of God, the rules and customs of the old kingdom no longer apply. He offered a new perspective and a point of entry into the new kingdom, the kingdom of God.

Those of us who have committed our lives to Jesus sometimes act as if we're still members of the old kingdom. It's as if our hearts have not yet made the transition into the kingdom of God. We expect our external, earthly world to change for the better—but the old kingdom is not part of the new one. We live in a world where these two kingdoms conflict, and the matter will not be resolved until the return of Christ. We are members of a new kingdom, temporarily lodging in the old kingdom. Until we fully reach the new kingdom, we must expect hardship and strife. Yet we can be content knowing that this life is a passing thought compared to eternity in heaven. On earth, we are "a mist that appears for a little while and then vanishes" (James 4:14).

Jesus demonstrated contentedness and peace when He faced Pontius Pilate and His imminent crucifixion, which of course, confounded Pilate. When asked if He was a king, Jesus replied, "My kingdom is not of this world. If it were, my servants would fight to prevent my arrest by the Jews. But now my kingdom is from another place" (John 18:36). We must assume that the early Christians—when the Roman emperor Nero fed them to dogs, nailed them to crosses, or used them as human torches to light his gardens in the evening—were equally content, because their executions inspired more martyrs and a rapidly expanding church. They also understood

Paul's secret—that trusting God, no matter how awful the circumstances, leads to peace and strength now and glory for eternity.

I don't mean to suggest, of course, that we should become blasé about the evils in the world around us. The Lord wants us as His followers to shine His light in all corners of darkness. We are to offer His love and hope to hurting people in every neighborhood, every city, and every nation. There is kingdom work to be done.

Yet if we can let go of the expectation that we will achieve harmony between this world and the next, and that our struggles in this life will one day disappear, then we can more easily find our way to greater trust in Him. This is part of His plan. It's hard, but it is good.

A Question of Justice

An overweight man sat at a round kitchen table, a cup of coffee in one hand and a cigarette in the other. A woman with her own cup of coffee sat across from him.

"He's a crook, that's what he is," the man said. "If he'd given us half of what we deserved, things would be different around here."

The woman nodded. "Mom's just as much to blame," she said. "He was always her favorite. We were the black sheep."

The man at the table was named Bob. The woman was his sister. They were discussing the recent death of their mother and the way their brother, Eldon, had swindled them. Before their mother died, Eldon persuaded her to sign over all her possessions to him, making him the executor of her estate. When she died, he sold everything—the house, the furniture, the cars, the rental properties, even an organ. It was all gone, along with the money from the sales.

So was Eldon—he'd disappeared.

Bob had been a practical joker all his life. But lately, the jokes came less frequently, often replaced by angry outbursts. As he talked to his sister, his face grew red and taut, his jaw set. The decibels of the voices flying back and forth across the kitchen table increased. Suddenly, Bob pounded the table so hard the silverware jumped.

"I wish I knew where he was," Bob said. "I'd like to get my hands on him just once. He's ruined my life. I just want a few minutes to ruin his too."[4]

Bob felt angry and bitter. I can't blame him for his anger—in his shoes, I'd have been angry too. But he allowed his anger to boil over into one of the most harmful conditions in human existence. As we saw in chapter 3, bitterness eats away at us until we're disillusioned and joyless. It usually damages us far more than the original crime itself did. Bitterness leaves us uneasy, upset, and far from Paul's state of being "content in any and every situation" (Phil. 4:12)

Why do we hold on to bitterness? Many times, we hang on to it because we want justice. We expect life to be fair. And if we've been wronged, we want the wrongdoer to suffer, to pay for the transgression.

Those are understandable sentiments. However, God intends for us to take a different approach and leave the matter of justice in His hands. Paul wrote, "If it is possible, as far as it depends on you, live at peace with everyone. Do not take revenge, my friends, but leave room for God's wrath, for it is written: 'It is mine to avenge; I will repay,' says the Lord" (Rom. 12:18–19).

We don't like that so much. We want to be part of the wrath. We want the satisfaction of being there when justice is meted out. Once again, God asks us to let go, surrender, and trust.

Actually, He asks even more. Scripture is quite clear that when someone has offended us, our responsibility is to forgive that person, "not seven times, but seventy-seven times" (Matt. 18:22). That can get really tough. How do we forgive a husband or wife who's had an affair? Who wants to forgive a rapist? The Lord's commands bring us right back to the precipice. It's so easy to say, "Forget it, God. I've been hurt too deeply. I'm not going to forgive. You're asking too much." And then walk away.

Don't do it.

Why? Because God doesn't insist on forgiveness for the sake of the perpetrator (though He cares about the soul of that person too). He wants you to forgive that person because He loves *you* and knows what bitterness will do to you if you hold on to it. So He's asking you to remove the poison, to let go of the pain. If you genuinely accept what's happened and move deeper into your trust in Him, you'll gain a strength and peace you never knew before. You'll experience a deeper level of His power and love.

I also urge you to remember that sometimes the hardest person of all to forgive is yourself. This goes back to our expectation of justice and fairness. If we're the one who's blown it—by having an affair or an abortion, by swindling someone, by gossiping, by losing our temper, whatever it may be—we may insist on mentally punishing ourselves, sometimes for years on end.

God's instructions for us are pretty clear in this case too. Yes, we are to take responsibility. We need to confess to God and, when possible, to the person we've injured. We need to make amends if we can and repent before the Lord. *And then we need to let it go.* Accept what's happened and accept the Lord's grace, because His willingness to forgive is a source of strength too: "Be strong in the grace that is in Christ Jesus" (2 Tim. 2:1).

Randy Alcorn has written, "Refusing to forgive ourselves is an act of pride—it's making ourselves and our sins bigger than God and His grace."[5] We're better off focusing on the Lord's commitment to forgiveness: "As far as the east is from the west, so far has he removed our transgressions from us" (Ps. 103:12).

Acceptance and trust.

Peace and strength.

They're yours for the choosing.

At the Precipice

About two weeks after the death of her daughter, Leslie McGill, still standing at the precipice, made her choice. Incredibly, while dealing with her grief, guilt, and loss, life had gotten even harder. The reason they'd just moved to Texas was for her husband's job, but the job was suddenly terminated. Not only that, but Leslie had developed a terrible case of poison ivy from crashing into the brush during the accident. A few people compared the McGills' plight to Job's.

Leslie didn't understand why things were happening the way they were. But she knew God wasn't mean-spirited. She realized that soon she needed to answer a question for herself: "Am I just playing at being a Christian, or do I *really* believe everything I taught my daughter?"

She recalls standing and talking with a friend when she put her decision into words. "I refuse to curse God and die," she said in a firm voice. "I am not going to do that."

Later, Leslie explained her thoughts at the time. "That was the moment for me," she says. "I knew I had to make a decision about what I was going to do with what had happened. I knew it was a life or death decision. I was thinking, *I am going to choose what everybody probably thinks is crazy and continue to be obedient and love God, even though the world thinks He just took my daughter. It's difficult enough to survive this with Him. There is no way I can do this without Him.*"

Her choice felt even more right as the days and weeks passed and Leslie reflected on the Lord's mercy. One example was the strange statement by eight-year-old Gabriel at the accident scene: "It's okay. If she's dead, it's all part of God's plan." At the time, Leslie hadn't said anything to her son about her fear that Marissa was already gone. Today, Gabriel doesn't remember saying anything. Leslie believes now that the Lord allowed an angel or Marissa herself to speak through her son in that moment.

Leslie also realized that every prayer she'd ever made on behalf of her daughter was now answered. Marissa was happy. Loved. At peace. Forever safe. She was with the only man who would ever be good enough for her. Leslie no longer had to wonder or worry about where her daughter was.

She also saw the Lord's hand in a ministry that took shape as the result of Marissa's death, one that will fulfill one of her daughter's dreams. Marissa's House is building an orphanage in Jimma, Ethiopia.

Leslie still has bad moments and days. She misses her daughter terribly. And she struggles with her identity. Before, she was Marissa and Gabriel's mom. Sometimes she feels as if half of her died in the crash. Yet she's grateful that her relationship with the Lord is more alive than it's ever been.

"My faith has definitely grown and strengthened," Leslie says. "I do feel closer to Him now. I can say that He provides amazing grace and mercy in the midst of the most horrible things. I'm trying to walk with Him at all times, to be thankful at all times, to live my life as an act of worship.

"I am trying to find Him in the dark places. Because I can't make it without Him."[6]

Chapter 7

Authentic Joy

There I was, stuck in the world's worst traffic jam. Beater cars, scooters, rickshaws, bicyclists, and pedestrians all competed for space on a narrow dirt road filled with potholes. Our car moved another three feet, then stopped. The early evening sun was still out, but you wouldn't know it. The smog was too thick.

I was in Jakarta, Indonesia, at the end of a grueling, three-week overseas business trip. I'd been sick in China from some kind of food poisoning and hadn't slept well for days. Now, after landing about 5:00 p.m. at the airport, I felt exhausted. The driver took me on the "scenic route" to my hotel. I sat in the back of a Mercedes-Benz (not that I appreciated the comfortable ride) and looked over my notes, preparing for my next meeting. I thought, *Lord, I can't do this. I want to be home with my wife. I want to hang out at the YMCA, play basketball, and have fun. Actually, I'm so tired, I just want to go to bed.*

You could say that I had a bad attitude.

Now, I'm not often aware of an immediate and direct response to my prayers—especially when they're as whiny as the one above—but on that day in Jakarta, I sensed an abrupt answer from the Lord.

Look up.

I looked up.

Outside my window, I saw five young boys playing in a puddle of black water a few feet away. They wore shorts and tattered shirts, some of the shirts missing all of their buttons and open down the front. Most of the boys walked around barefoot. They squatted down, pushing dented Coca-Cola cans across the murky liquid as if they were little toy ships on an ocean.

What surprised me, however, was how much fun they were having. I could see them giggling and laughing with each other.

Then the one closest to the car noticed me staring at them. He said something to the others, then all five broke into some of the biggest smiles I'd ever seen, their white teeth contrasting sharply with their grimy faces. Some actually jumped up and down with excitement.

The kids ran to our car, which was still barely moving, waved hello, and slapped their hands on my window. I rolled the window down, and we exchanged "Hi's." They weren't looking for money and never put a hand out. They were just having fun and enjoying a moment with an interested stranger. As we slowly pulled away, I looked back over my shoulder. They gave me a final wave, then turned back for more "boat" races in the dirty puddle.

We continued to inch our way forward, but my mind was no longer on the traffic. I sensed the Lord telling me something. It was as if He said to me, "*They* seem joyful. What's *your* problem?"

God-Centered Joy

We've already covered a lot of ground in this book. We've talked about choosing the broken road that leads to God and greater strength. We've also explored some forks in the trail that offer more choices. When we choose well, the paths of surrender, relationship, acceptance, and trust lead us even closer to Him and His power.

Now we're standing in front of another fork. This time, we're seeking a path that will deliver us to something we're all looking for: *joy*. What's interesting, however, is that the trail to joy is unmarked, full of rocks and overgrown weeds, and rarely traveled. As a result, whenever we arrive at this fork, we almost always choose the wrong path—and end up wondering why we're lost.

To put it in plain terms, we often think possessions and things will make us happy. Food. Sex. Money. A new dress, couch, car, home, job, or spouse. We think that if we rearrange the circumstances, everything will get better. Eventually, some of us figure out, at least some of the time, that this isn't how it works. The external possessions and things are enticing and may offer temporary pleasure, but ultimately, they don't make a difference. They are the wrong path.

Joy springs from an internal choice—a decision of the heart about the heart. It has nothing to do with circumstances and everything to do with God and where we are going with Him. It also—and this is the part that trips us up—has little to do with what we, in all our "wisdom," want and believe we need. The path that leads to joy is based entirely on what God desires for us. Once we begin to walk in the direction He's pointing out to us, we discover true delight.

Said another way, joy results when we focus more on God and less—as I failed to do that day in Jakarta—on ourselves.

You may recall that when Peter and the other apostles began preaching, teaching, and healing after the death and resurrection of Jesus, they were arrested and brought before the Sanhedrin, the Jewish supreme court. The apostles had ignored the Sanhedrin's order to stop teaching in the name of Christ.

When pressed for an explanation, Peter and the others responded, "We must obey God rather than men! The God of our fathers raised Jesus from the dead—whom you had killed by hanging him on a tree" (Acts 5:29–30).

The Sanhedrin officials were furious at these words and wanted to put the apostles to death. A Pharisee spoke and persuaded them to abandon their plan. Instead, they had the apostles flogged, ordered them to stop teaching, and released them.

Did Peter and the rest slink away in relief at their narrow escape? Did they tremble after their brush with death? *Not even close.* Instead, "The apostles left the Sanhedrin, rejoicing because they had been counted worthy of suffering disgrace for the Name" (Acts 5:41). And they went right back to teaching and proclaiming the good news.

Think about it. You have a confrontation with the leading officials of the day that nearly ends with a death sentence. Men flog you with whips—we're talking about serious physical pain here. The officials order you to stop what you're doing, and yet you know in your heart that you won't stop, and that more confrontations and trouble are in your future.

And you walk away rejoicing.

That makes no sense from a me-centered perspective. The "me" in this case isn't faring so well in the present, and the future doesn't look too bright either.

If the perspective shifts from "me" to God, however, everything changes.

Choosing the Right Trail

I know of an eleven-year-old boy who recently had an interesting encounter with these two perspectives. A neighbor family was selling chocolate chip cookies—two for a dollar—and since the boy (his name was Peter too) just happened to have a buck in his pocket, he bought two. At that moment, his perspective was very much centered on "me." He felt happier because he was looking forward to eating those cookies!

When Peter rode his bike home, he found his dad working on something in the garage. His dad looked tired. Suddenly, Peter's perspective shifted. He knew how much his dad liked chocolate chip cookies.

"Here, Dad," Peter said, handing over one of his treasures. "I just bought two cookies. You can have one."

"Thanks, Peter," his dad said with a smile. "That's very thoughtful of you."

Peter smiled back. Strangely enough, even though he was down to just one cookie, he felt even more joy than when he had two cookies.

About an hour later, however, the cookies were gone, and Peter started thinking about what else he could buy from the neighbors. After spending his dollar, all he had left was loose change. Peter's perspective was changing again.

Pretty soon, Peter found his father still in the garage. "Hey, Dad," he said. "Remember that cookie I gave you? You owe me fifty cents!"

Isn't this what a lot of us struggle with when we stand at that fork in the road? We're looking for happiness, but we're a little confused about which trail will lead to the lasting joy we desire. Even when we're on the right trail, we're just as likely to backtrack and pick the wrong path than stay on the trail to genuine joy.

If you're lost in the forest of life or trying to choose from two paths, just remember that there are no pictures of *you* on your map to joy. You'll find your way by examining the world around you and asking yourself a few questions: *Who do I know who's in need today? Who could use a meal, help with yard work, an hour of babysitting, a word of encouragement, someone to listen to, or a shoulder to cry on?* Amazingly, when you help lift someone else's burden, you'll find that the effort lifts yours as well.

As useful and uplifting as that is, however, the first step in finding your way to joy is the incredibly important and often forgotten act of offering praise to the Lord.

The Guy in the Mirror

Praise and worship are important to our heavenly Father. The Lord says in Scripture, "the people I formed for myself that they may proclaim my praise" (Isa. 43:21), and "Worship the Lord your God, and serve him only" (Matt. 4:10).

Do our praise and worship bring Him glory and pleasure? *Yes.* But the benefit is ours as well: "Praise the LORD. How good it is to sing praises to our God, how pleasant and fitting to praise him!" (Ps. 147:1).

We "get" this on Sunday mornings. We memorize the lyrics to hymns and worship songs and belt them out, impressing our pew-mates with our volume and enthusiasm (if not always with the quality of our singing). We shout (or at least think loudly) our hallelujahs to the heavens. We leave the church proclaiming glory to God in the highest.

But how are we the rest of the week? What happens to the quality of our praise and worship when we're alone? How do we respond when the boss says no to a raise request or when a toddler dumps his cereal on the floor for the fifth time or when a best friend dies? Do we still praise God when we're so lonely that we don't think we can face another morning?

I remember a day when I was especially low emotionally. It was about a year after I'd graduated from college. I was working in San Diego as a sales rep for a company that made envelopes. My sister Dee Dee and I were renting a two-bedroom townhouse. I was home for lunch in my suit and tie, alone, staring into the bathroom mirror. Staring back was a discouraged and confused individual. Sure, I'd dedicated my life to the Lord a few years before. But I was still figuring out just what that meant for me. I dreamed of a life of meaning, but at that moment, I felt incredibly empty.

Lord, I prayed, *what am I doing? Is this what life is about? I'm just a cog in the system, working from eight to six and trying to make a living. What do You want from me? What do I need to do? Is this all You have for me?*

The guy in the mirror was losing hope.

It occurred to me in that moment that I was totally immersed in what was happening—or actually, *not happening*—in my life. I didn't see a clear path to the future, and I was letting it destroy my present.

Okay, I thought, *it doesn't have to be this way. I'm not going to let my circumstances dictate my feelings.*

I decided that it was time for drastic action—I needed to start singing songs of praise to God. I say "drastic" because I wasn't much into music at the time, and I was a terrible singer. I didn't know any worship-song melodies or words, so I just started making them up.

"God, You are an awesome God," I sang. "You are the King of Kings, the Lord of Lords. You have my life in Your hands." As I sang, something strange happened. I felt an overwhelming and wonderful change inside, as if someone had poured a bucket of joy on top of me. It spread throughout my body until I was literally filled with an intense sensation of bliss. I felt the Lord's presence; I felt that everything was going to be all right. I'd never experienced anything like it before.

Pretty soon, I was doing more than singing. Right there in the bathroom, and out into the bedroom, I started dancing. I really couldn't help myself. I wanted to honor the Lord in every way. God was in control, and I was just enjoying the ride.

Finally, I looked back in the mirror and smiled. The guy in front of me didn't appear anything like the forlorn fellow I'd seen a few minutes before.

"Okay, Lord," I said, "I'm just going to go finish my day. We're going to have fun."

A few years later, I read about King David bringing the ark of God to his city, where he celebrated and "danced before the LORD with all his might" (2 Sam. 6:14). It reminded me of my moment in front of the bathroom mirror in San Diego. David was a man who made many mistakes—murder and adultery are as big as they get—yet he is regarded repeatedly in Scripture as "a man after [God's] own heart" (Acts 13:22). David was far from perfect, but he got the main message—life is about God, not us.

I'm not holding myself up as an example to follow because I'm also far from perfect. Yet during that discouraging afternoon in San Diego, I believe I made the choice God wanted me to make. In the middle of my misery, I decided to praise Him for who He is. The Lord responded and blessed me with what I would describe as a searing joy. What is perhaps more amazing is that despite many bumps and frustrations and crises over the twenty-five years since that day, I've never had another emotional low like that one. The credit is all His.

God has good reasons for telling us in Scripture, "Rejoice in the Lord always. I will say it again: Rejoice!" (Phil. 4:4). If we take Him at His word and *always* rejoice in Him, we can discover the power of God-centered joy.

The Joy Set Before Him

When my son Trenton was born, I was in shock. I think for many guys, the birth of our first child is the moment we cease being children ourselves and become men. After seventeen-and-a-half hours of labor, Jean was thrilled but exhausted. She needed sleep. I felt wired by the whole experience. *Wow!* I thought. *We just had a baby!*

I remember the nurse bringing Trent back into our room shortly after his birth. I took him and, as Jean slept, held him in the rocking chair alongside Jean's bed for the entire night. I prayed for him, I sang to him, I made him promises about being a good dad. The troubles of my childhood were the furthest thing from my mind. I felt an indescribable joy—*this is my son!*

This is what Jesus was talking about when He said to the disciples, "A woman giving birth to a child has pain because her time has come; but when her baby is born she forgets the anguish because of her joy that a child is born into this world" (John 16:21). I can only imagine that kind of pain, but I'm certain that forgetting it requires a powerful joy. That's the kind of joy I want in my life.

We can see another kind of joy demonstrated by the believers of the early church in Macedonia. Paul writes of the Macedonians, "Out of the most severe trial, their overflowing joy and their extreme poverty welled up in rich generosity" (2 Cor. 8:2).

Take another look at that verse. These people struggled with a severe trial, probably the extreme poverty that Paul mentions. They weren't just poor—they were *extremely* poor. They had less than nothing. And yet they experienced "overflowing joy," and because of that joy they "gave as much as they were able, and even beyond their ability. Entirely on their own, they urgently pleaded with us for the privilege of sharing in this service to the saints" (2 Cor. 8:3–4).

Kind of makes you scratch your head, right?

If I asked if you wanted to trade places right now with those early church Macedonians, would you do it? Extreme poverty doesn't sound all that appealing. Yet these people were happy to the point that it was *overflowing*. How many of us, with all our material advantages, can say that?

Only those experiencing a powerful, godly joy would say they are happy to the point of overflowing.

In another passage of Scripture, Paul writes, "Let us fix our eyes on Jesus, the author and perfecter of our faith, who for the joy set before him endured the cross, scorning its shame, and sat down at the right hand of the throne of God. Consider him who endured such opposition from sinful men, so that you will not grow weary and lose heart" (Heb. 12:2–3).

What was it that allowed Jesus in His humanity to endure the taunts and schemes of sinful men and an agonizing death while nailed to a wooden cross? What propelled Him to heaven to sit at the right hand of the throne of God?

The joy set before Him.

When Paul instructs us to keep this example in mind when we are discouraged and oppressed, what is he saying? It's the *joy set before us* that will send us to victory.

If we keep the joy of eternity at the forefront of our minds, the nagging problems and traumatic incidents that so often disrupt our lives don't deliver quite the same sting. I'm not talking about the kind of happiness that comes from buying a new plasma TV. I am talking about a deep, abiding, and lasting joy—a joy that will triumph over the most deceitful people we'll ever encounter, the most terrible pain, and even death itself.

A Time to Laugh

Life is often funny. Yes, it takes all kinds of unexpected twists and turns that we never quite figure out. But if we look at it from a certain viewpoint, life can be downright hilarious.

Take the case of a hockey player named Phil Callaway. As a young boy, Phil dreamed of being a star on the ice. He imagined competing with the greats of the game: Gordie Howe, Frank Mahovlich, Bobby Orr. Soon, Phil was old enough to play in real hockey arenas, and he pursued his life's dream with gusto. His teams, unfortunately, weren't very good. He was in tenth grade before he landed on a squad with a winning record.

Phil's performance on that team, however, produced a memory that will live forever when people tell stories about the Callaway clan.

It was late March. Through an amazing combination of good fortune and good play, Phil's team had reached the championship game. The small arena was packed. Phil had a feeling that this was going to be his night.

With a minute left in the game, however, Phil's hopes of glory were on the verge of extinction. His squad trailed 3–2. That's when Phil went to work. A teammate in the corner passed him the puck. Phil maneuvered into position and rifled a shot at the net. The goalie dove … *and missed.*

The red light went on. Girls screamed and cheered.

The game was tied, and Phil Callaway was a hero. The only thing left to complete Phil's dream night was to score the winning goal in overtime.

Now Phil could really feel it. While waiting in the dressing room before the overtime period, he peeked out at the crowd.

Prepare yourselves, you lucky people, he thought. *Tonight, destiny is on my side. Tonight will be* my *night. You will remember me for years to come.*

Five minutes later, Phil's moment arrived. It seemed to unfold in slow motion. The puck slipped across the ice toward the open net. Phil made his move, diving onto the ice. He swung his stick, striking the puck and sending it past the goal line.

Once again, the red light flicked on and girls screamed.

This time, though, they weren't cheering.

Phil had scored into his own net.

Phil's father had missed the game because of the flu. Later that night, when Phil arrived home, his dad stood in the doorway of Phil's bedroom. "How did it go?" he asked.

"Aw, Dad," Phil said. "I can't tell you. You're sick enough."

Soon, though, the story spilled out ... every last embarrassing detail.

For a minute, Phil's father sat on the bed next to his son, saying nothing. Then he put his hand on Phil's knee.

And then he began to laugh.

To his surprise, Phil started laughing with him. And suddenly, unexpectedly, the anguish and humiliation began to melt away.[1]

I think the Lord has a sense of humor, and I believe that our ability to laugh is a gift from Him. Science tells us that there are health benefits to laughter. Laurence Gonzales, in his book *Deep Survival: Who Lives, Who Dies, and Why,* writes:

> Laughter stimulates the left prefrontal cortex, an area in the brain that helps us to feel good and to be motivated. That stimulation alleviates anxiety and frustration. There is evidence that laughter can send chemical signals to actively inhibit the firing of nerves in the amygdala, thereby dampening fear. Laughter, then, can help to temper negative emotions.[2]

Since He made us, God knew all about the power of laughter. This is why we're told in Scripture that there is "a time to weep and a time to laugh" (Eccl. 3:4). Jesus also tells us, "Blessed are you who weep now, for you will laugh" (Luke 6:21). So the Lord is okay with laughing. He planned for it and expects it.

If we can learn to find humor in life's difficult moments, we'll be better equipped to take on the truly frightening and tragic events that come our way. Humor doesn't erase the bad times, but it sure makes them easier to bear.

A good laugh is like a little window into heaven and the joy that's waiting for us there. I don't know about you, but the thought of that makes me smile.

Dealing with Depression

I recognize that for many people, the decision to choose laughter or joy is not as simple as turning on a light switch. We can be trapped so deep in the pit of despair that it's impossible to climb out without help. Despite the dysfunction of my own family situation, I never really experienced this level of unending hopelessness while growing up. I attribute that to God, the way He made me, and a realistic attitude about people and the world that prevented me from being crushed by continuing disappointment.

As an adult, however, I began to develop an appreciation for what so many deal with every day. I'm talking about depression, and my first inkling of its devastating effects appeared during the second year of my marriage. After brushing my teeth one night, I climbed into bed, only to discover that Jean was sobbing. Unsure what had provoked such deep, heartfelt tears, I asked, "What's wrong?"

Brushing away the tears, she said, "I just don't think you should stay married to me." As we talked, I realized that a big part of what Jean wrestled with that night was depression.

This issue hit home during a later conversation I had with Jean. I've always been a person who, when things get really tough, has been able to dig down and, with the Lord's help, find a way to keep going. Again, I don't take credit for this. There is a concept in the field of psychology called resilience theory. It attempts to explain why some people go through trauma, perhaps even for decades, yet live relatively normal and stable lives. I seem to fit this profile, and I think it's a gift from the Lord.

But I was unaware that many people struggle with optimism. Jean expressed it to me one day after I "encouraged" her to move past what was troubling her. "Jim, some of us just *can't* pull ourselves up by our bootstraps and get going." It was an "aha" moment for me. It gave me a new appreciation for what Jean and so many others, including believers, are struggling with.

I've learned that approximately fifteen million adults in the United States—roughly 8 percent of the population over the age of eighteen—deal with major depression in a given year. Women experience depression about twice as often as men, and over their lifetime, about 12 percent of women will have what would be diagnosed as clinical depression. What's even more alarming is that approximately 80 percent of people who are experiencing depression are not receiving any treatment.[3]

Jean can speak to this issue from the inside. I'll let her tell her story:

> I struggle with depression. During the early years of
> our marriage, when Jim realized what I was dealing
> with, he asked me to go to a counselor. I reluctantly

went to one appointment and told him I couldn't go back. The idea of needing counseling made me feel like a failure.

Then, when I was thirty-one, my lovable thirty-three-year-old brother committed suicide, and depression took me deeper into its grip. It was the most difficult thing I have ever faced. The depth of my despair seemed bottomless. The blackness and hopelessness were crushing.

I did not see how I could continue living. I believe that God does not give us more than we can handle, yet my brother's death utterly felt like more than I could handle. Suicide was not an option—I could not add to my family's overwhelming pain— so I felt sure the Lord was going to take my life, maybe in a car accident.

But I didn't die. I knew then that I had to do something and that I needed help. That's when I started going to Christian counseling.

For me, counseling has been a very positive experience. It's been hard and forced me to explore a number of tough issues, but it's changed my life in valuable ways. I still struggle. I am not healed. But I live with hope.

After I started counseling, I had a new obstacle to overcome when my counselor suggested I go on antidepressant medication. Once again, I was devastated. I experienced an intense feeling of failure as a Christian and a human being. I felt I was being labeled as mentally ill. It was a year or two before I was ready to accept the idea that medication could help me.

There is a stigma surrounding antidepressants, and it may be that they are overprescribed in our country—some people, encouraged by doctors and counselors, turn to medication as a way to avoid dealing with issues in their lives. But there is also a stigma at the other end of the spectrum. We may think we are weak or lack faith because we need antidepressants, and therefore, some of us view antidepressant medication differently than insulin or chemotherapy. Yet for many, antidepressants address a chemical imbalance and are a legitimate solution to a terrible problem.

Part of me believes that if I spend more time reading the Bible, praying, focusing on others instead of myself, exercising regularly, and eating well, then all my depression will eventually disappear. While these are necessary and helpful elements to healing, peace, and contentment, in some cases more is needed.

What I've learned through my own experience and through talking to experts in the field is that when we are struggling with major depression, we can spiral down into a vicious cycle. In the grip of that cycle, we don't have the energy to do the very things that will help us. For some of us, medication and Christian counseling help dig us out of that pit so we can feel alive enough to interact meaningfully with others, exercise, pursue a hobby, pray, or volunteer. Another way we can help improve our emotional outlook is to schedule breaks for relaxation rather than waiting until we are exhausted. Reading a good book or listening to uplifting or soothing music or to the Bible on CD or iPod can also help lift our spirits.

Depression may be my "thorn in my flesh." I don't know if I will ever be completely healed, but I do know that God wants me to turn to Him—to talk to Him and read His Word. When you're depressed, you get to a point where the only place to turn is God—which is exactly what He wants. He desires a relationship with us.

I remember a time after my brother's suicide when Jim said to me, "Scripture says that good will come from this."

I believe every word of the Bible and know it is the inerrant Word of God. But that day, I didn't see the potential for anything positive. I shook my finger at Jim and said, "Nothing good can ever come from this!"

I wouldn't have believed it at the time, but I was wrong. While God did not want my brother to die, and I would give anything to have him back, now I see how the Lord used his death for good in my life. It forced me to go to counseling and face issues I'd been unwilling to face. It gave me a new depth of feeling and compassion for people in pain and has allowed me to talk to other people about depression and encourage them. It's helped me realize what is truly important in life and strive to free myself from superfluous things.

And it has deepened my relationship with the Lord. Through my brother's death and my own experience with depression, I now know that true contentment and peace can only come from a relationship with Christ.

If you are reading this and struggle with depression, please know that there is light at the end of the tunnel. God understands and desires to transform your pain. He loves each of us more than we can ever imagine. He wants us to be filled with His peace and joy.[4]

I'm so proud of Jean for how she's allowed the Lord to work in her heart—and for her openness in sharing this with you. If you need to talk to someone about depression, please don't stay silent. Speak with your pastor or a trusted friend, or call Focus on the Family at 1-800-A-FAMILY (1-800-232-6459). We have a staff of licensed, professional Christian counselors available to talk with you.

A Dump in Cairo

If there is a secret to discovering and staying on the "joy trail" that extends from the path of brokenness, I think it's found in the final instructions Paul wrote in a letter to the members of the early church at the seaport city of Thessalonica: "Be joyful always; pray continually; give thanks in all circumstances, for this is God's will for you in Christ Jesus" (1 Thess. 5:16–18).

I find great hope in these verses. Paul begins by saying we are to always be joyful. I believe this implies that no matter what's going on in our life, joy *is* possible—and that if we don't have it, we need to do something about it!

The next two phrases tell us how to get that joy. First, Paul encourages us to pray continually. That means we should be constantly talking with God, telling Him about our feelings and problems. If the Lord is our source of abiding joy, then the more active we are in our relationship with Him, the easier it will be to draw on His joy and strength.

Second, he says we are to give thanks in all circumstances. In other words, while we're praying and talking with God, we need to make sure we thank Him for the blessings He's provided, no matter how bleak our situation. The words "all circumstances" implies that even in the most desperate of times, we can find reasons to be thankful. Our future in eternity with Jesus is a good place to start.

Finally, Paul reminds us that joyfulness is God's will for us. Joy isn't a state of mind that we pursue only when we're in the mood. It's not an extra bonus that's added to our life like sprinkles on an ice cream sundae. This is a command from the Lord: *Be joyful!*

Because of the many business trips I've taken overseas during my career, I've had the opportunity to observe a variety of peoples and cultures. I've been struck by how often those with very few possessions seem happier than those with many. I don't think that's just a comment on the dangers of materialism. It's also, in my opinion, a demonstration of the idea that those who have no other "distractions" find it easier to draw close to our heavenly Father and the joy He offers to each and every one of us.

About ten years ago, I was with some colleagues in Cairo, Egypt, on a Focus on the Family business trip. We were visiting a dump at the edge of the city as part of an ongoing ministry there. Our mission was to hand out blankets, shoes, and candy to kids, but I spent much of my time simply observing. What I saw was both heartwrenching and heartwarming.

On our drive to the dump, our car weaved through dusty dirt roads littered with mounds of garbage. Red brick buildings two and three stories high lined the streets, though many of the brick walls had crumbled and the windows were no longer filled with glass. It wasn't a pretty scene.

Finally, we arrived at our destination. The dump itself was a crater roughly a hundred yards wide, filled with bags, bottles, broken glass, and every kind of trash imaginable, surrounded by a circular berm. The stench was unforgettable. Wild dogs roamed everywhere. My eyes were drawn, however, to the flimsy shacks that circled the berm of trash. They were shanties, really, probably six feet wide and twelve feet deep, made of cardboard and plastic taped or simply pressed together. These were the homes of the Christian believers who had no place else to go.

It's difficult for many Christians in a Muslim nation such as Egypt to find work or reasonable housing. That was the case for the families at the dump. They had so few options that they resorted to searching through every new truckload of trash, hoping to find treasures to wear, barter with, sell, or even eat.

It seemed a grim existence.

We got out of our cars and began distributing our gifts. One little girl no more than five years old caught my attention. She wore a torn pink sweater, a tattered shirt, and shorts, and hid behind her mother's equally worn dress. As we adults talked, she popped into view every few moments to peek at me. She had huge brown eyes, and when I handed her some candy, she displayed an even bigger smile.

In fact, just about everyone in the dump wore huge smiles. The parents deeply appreciated our gifts, continually saying (through an interpreter), "Thank you. It's good to be with you today. It's good to have you here." Many looked as thin as the clothes they wore. Most of the adults had no teeth. None of that stopped them from smiling ear to ear.

I sensed it was more than gratitude for our gifts. These people were content. They felt a deep peace. They understood that there was a purpose to their existence. Nearly all of the families were intact—a mom and a dad, living with their children. Something was going on here that much of the world has missed. When I looked in the faces of those Cairo Christians, I saw joy.

That Your Joy May Be Complete

Where does your happiness come from? Does your joy depend on your status in life, the kind of day you're having, your health, or even the weather? Or does your happiness and joy come from something deeper? To receive the full measure of the joy the Lord wants to give us, we've got to put all our hope and trust in Him.

On the night of His arrest in the garden of Gethsemane, Jesus said the following words to the disciples:

> "As the Father has loved me, so have I loved you. Now remain in my love. If you obey my commands, you will remain in my love, just as I have obeyed my Father's commands and remain in his love. I have told you this so that my joy may be in you and that your joy may be complete." (John 15:9–11)

Our heavenly Father is offering His love and joy to us every day, and we can know it by seeking Him and His will.

My prayer is that you won't settle for the fleeting moments of happiness that this world promotes. Instead, I hope that you discover authentic *joy*—which is powerful, complete, and eternal.

PART 3

Chapter 8

Strength through Perseverance

By now, I hope our discussions have led you to the same amazing conclusion I've reached—that there is an unmistakable connection between trials and godly strength. As hard as it may be to accept, I believe we've discovered that the key to success in this life—*success from God's perspective*—is found in the choices we make when we encounter obstacles and persecution.

There is both opportunity and purpose in our suffering. Every time we come to that fork in the road and choose the trail that the Lord intends, we move closer to Him and His love and strength. It doesn't mean we'll find an easier life, but it does make us more capable of handling the next challenge—and better equipped to serve our heavenly Father.

I don't know about you, but I get excited when I stop and allow the significance of this message to sink in. I suppose the reason for this is it gives me hope. It reminds me that God finds a way to use the twists in life's road that have brought me to this point, and He's

going to keep on using those curves as I go forward. I admit it: I
don't mind when life is running as smoothly as a finely tuned engine.
But it's nice to know that the painful moments and experiences are
more than just detours slowing me from reaching my destination. I
believe they're actually road signs to the future the Lord has precisely
planned for me.

The hope I'm talking about is the same hope that Paul refers to
in his letter to the early Christians in Rome. In it, he explains salvation to a church that has not received the instruction of an apostle
before. He also explains something that, once again, appears to make
little sense at first glance. He says that suffering is the foundation of
our strength because it is the first step toward hope.

> We rejoice in the hope of the glory of God. Not
> only so, but we also rejoice in our sufferings,
> because we know that suffering produces perse-
> verance; perseverance, character; and character,
> hope. And hope does not disappoint us, because
> God has poured out his love into our hearts by
> the Holy Spirit, whom he has given us. (Rom.
> 5:2–5)

Don't miss this progression: suffering, then perseverance, then
character, then hope—a hope that may be the most powerful weapon
any of us will ever wield.

Is this a foolproof formula? A guarantee? Not at all. I know
plenty of people who have suffered, gone the other direction, and
lost hope in the process. So what *is* the Lord telling us here through

Paul's words? Let's talk about it in the next three chapters and see what comes alive in our hearts.

Persevering through the Pain

Stormie Omartian, the author and singer, knows something about pain and suffering. When she was a child, her mentally ill mother often kept her locked in a closet. As if that wasn't bad enough, her mother rejected her, telling Stormie she would grow up to be a failure.

When Stormie married her husband, producer Michael Omartian, the pain did not end. Michael, a perfectionist, struggled with his temper, and Stormie responded to any harsh words and criticism by retreating mentally and emotionally. She prayed for their marriage and her husband, but the prayer usually consisted of three words: "Change him, Lord!" This pattern continued for nearly fifteen years.

Many marriages today would not survive five years under these conditions, let alone almost fifteen. Yet even though nothing seemed to be changing, Stormie persevered. Was her faith in God a factor in her perseverance? Of course. But I also can't help thinking that her traumatic experiences as a child gave her additional perspective and power. I believe that the pain of those years helped open her heart to wait on the Lord and gave her additional strength to hold out for something better in her marriage, instead of cutting loose.

The day came when Stormie reached her limit. In her bedroom, she cried out in desperation to the Lord. "God, I can't live this way anymore," she pleaded. "I know what You've said about divorce, but I can't live in the same house with him. Help me, Lord!"

Sitting there on her bed, Stormie felt a strong temptation to gather her children and leave for good. Yet she didn't. She was willing to listen to whatever the Lord had to tell her. Soon, she sensed Him showing her what a new life would be like without her husband. She also sensed what a legacy of divorce would mean for her kids. It was a sad picture. Stormie realized this wasn't the plan God had designed for her and her family.

Then Stormie felt a different response from the Lord. He was telling her that if she laid down her life in prayer for Michael, God would use her to help Michael become the man he was meant to be.

Stormie cried at this. It hurt. But in the end, she agreed and began praying for her husband in a new way. And little by little, the Lord began working changes—not only in Michael's heart, but also in Stormie's. Her perseverance, combined with prayer and God's mighty power, transformed their marriage. Today, after more than thirty years together, their relationship is stronger than they ever imagined it could be.[1]

I know of another family that practiced perseverance through a different kind of pain. A wife and husband in England raised one child, a daughter. To the shock of her parents, however, on her eighteenth birthday she left home and disappeared. Her parents were devastated. They didn't know if she was alive or dead.

As the months passed into years, her mother determined that she would leave the porch light on all night, every night. It was a message that she would always be welcomed back. It was also a way for the anguished mother to retain hope. Many nights, when she locked the front door and turned on the porch light, tears streamed down her face.

What the mother didn't know was that often her daughter was parked on the road in front of the house, staring at that single light still shining in the neighborhood. She wanted to come home but resisted because she felt she'd caused too much hurt.

Finally, six years after she'd left, the daughter walked back into her former home and her parents' lives. She also came home to God. Today, the daughter is happily married and has two sons who enjoy time with their grandparents.[2]

Would the daughter have come back if her mother had not turned on the porch light night after night? That's hard to answer. But I believe in the daughter's mind, the light emitted by that single bulb shone far brighter because she knew how much pain was behind it. The light meant more to her because of the suffering. For her, it was a beacon of perseverance and hope.

The power of perseverance, which can come through suffering, is available to all of us, no matter how old or how young we are. I was reminded of this when I visited a foster-home program (called Ithemba, which translates to "Place of Hope") in South Africa sponsored by Focus on the Family South Africa. While there I visited with a fifteen-year-old girl whose English name is Peaceful. Two years before, Peaceful had been in a desperate situation.

Her parents died from AIDS. She knew no other relatives or friends who could care for or protect her. Yet she couldn't give up—her sister, then ten years old, and brother, then seven, depended on her.

Peaceful's consuming desire was for her sister and brother to have a normal life. To feed them, she begged for food from neighbors. When there wasn't enough to go around, she went without. Many nights, all three of them went to bed with empty stomachs. Either way, each evening Peaceful gathered her siblings' clothes and washed them by hand with an old washboard and tub. It was something her mother did for her and a way to make her sister and brother feel that they were cared for and that life would go on.

The Lord honored Peaceful's perseverance when she and her sister and brother were welcomed as the first members of Ithemba's foster-care program in South Africa. To me, Peaceful is another example of amazing strength, born of suffering and refined by perseverance.

Rooted in Love

I've wondered about the spiritual implications of perseverance. What is it about our steadfastness that draws us closer to our heavenly Father? Why exactly is our stubborn refusal to give up such an admirable quality in the eyes of God?

We know that the Lord watches for and recognizes our perseverance. Jesus said, "I know your deeds, your love and faith, your service and perseverance, and that you are now doing more than you did at first" (Rev. 2:19).

We also know that the Lord honors our persistence, at least when the motivation is godly. Jesus told the parable of a widow who repeatedly approached a judge seeking justice against an adversary. The "unjust" judge didn't fear God or care about men, but he agreed to grant justice to the widow so he wouldn't have to deal with the woman further. Jesus said, "Listen to what the unjust judge says. And will not God bring about justice for his chosen ones, who cry out to him day and night? Will he keep putting them off? I tell you, he will see that they get justice, and quickly" (Luke 18:6–8).

In addition, we understand that God will bless our perseverance, particularly when it flourishes during times of trial. James wrote,

> Brothers, as an example of patience in the face of suffering, take the prophets who spoke in the name of the Lord. As you know, we consider blessed those who have persevered. You have heard of Job's perseverance and have seen what the Lord finally brought about. The Lord is full of compassion and mercy. (James 5:10–11)

Maybe what's most significant about our perseverance is that it is a tangible sign of our faith and love. Remember the promise that the Lord made to Abraham? He said that Abraham would become the father of a great nation. Those were unbelievable words for an old man and his barren wife to hear. And for more than twenty years after that promise, nothing happened.

Abraham surely wondered what was going on, but his faith in the Lord persevered: "He did not waver through unbelief regarding the promise of God, but was strengthened in his faith" (Rom. 4:20). And finally, when the time was right, the Lord blessed Abraham and Sarah with a son named Isaac (Gen. 21:2–3).

When we encounter someone else's perseverance that is framed by confusion and pain, isn't this what most moves our own hearts? If you've repeatedly hurt your spouse by ignoring her needs yet she responds with kindness … if you've lost your temper with your child many times over the years yet he still says, "I love you, Mommy" at the end of the day … if you've insulted a friend yet she stands by your side when you receive a cancer diagnosis … doesn't that cause you to melt inside? Doesn't it make you want to change your ways like nothing else?

There is life-transforming power in this kind of perseverance. It alters everyone who comes into contact with it. And ultimately, perseverance is rooted in love: "[Love] always protects, always trusts, always hopes, always perseveres" (1 Cor. 13:7).

The Slippery Slope

Our godly perseverance is important not only for what it can mean to us and those around us, but also because it keeps us away from the pit of darkness and despair.

In 2004, Drew Wills was an accomplished Colorado Springs attorney, happily married husband, father of two children in college, and avid bicyclist and outdoor enthusiast. On the second-to-last day of the year, he went on a ski outing with his family and brother at Aspen Highlands ski resort. Drew started down a familiar but steep ski run with heavy moguls. As he skied down the mountain, he saw a woman working her way sideways across the slope, apparently because she wasn't comfortable with the terrain. He realized the woman was moving directly into his path.

Drew, watching the woman, maneuvered to avoid her. His attention was drawn away for only a moment, but it was long enough to distract him from the large pine that stood apart from the rest of the tree line. An instant later, Drew spotted the pine and tried to turn, but it was too late. The impact of his lower body slamming into the tree spun him around in a complete circle.

Drew lay in the snow, trying to gather his senses. His back hurt like crazy, but otherwise he seemed to be okay. Then he looked down at his legs. His brain told him they looked just fine, stretched out straight in front of him. His eyes, however, showed his legs splayed out at strange angles to the side.

That's when Drew knew something was terribly wrong.

The accident had broken Drew's back and severed his spinal cord. He was paralyzed from the waist down.

For Drew, it was the beginning of a difficult journey to a new way of life. After evacuation off the mountain and a helicopter ride to a Grand Junction hospital, a surgeon inserted screws and two titanium rods to fuse his back. He was then flown to Englewood's Craig Hospital, a leading rehabilitation center.

Drew's first days at Craig included more than a few dark moments. Active and independent all his life, he was suddenly bed-ridden and receiving twenty-four-hour care. He had to adjust to the idea of being permanently dependent on others. He felt considerable pain and had to take a variety of medications. He couldn't sleep—the nurses turned him every two hours, and his roommate kept a TV blaring day and night.

Then he got sick. He'd never felt so awful. The doctors had theories, but they were unable to diagnose the problem.

Drew was already a man of faith. Almost from the moment of his accident, he had prayed. Now his petitions grew more urgent than ever.

"Lord, I'm not sure what I'm going to do here," he prayed. "Please take away the pain. Please help the doctors discover what's wrong so I can get healthy and learn to function again. Please don't leave me like this. You're all I've got."

Drew didn't understand why God had allowed this drastic detour in his life. Yet even in his worst moments, he never felt abandoned. He knew God was there with him, and he clung fiercely to that truth.

After a few days of misery, the doctors finally diagnosed Drew's illness—a urinary tract infection, which is relatively common for people with spinal cord injuries. As the proper medication took effect and Drew's infection receded, his spirits rose. They jumped higher when his son showed him photos of hand-cycles and other adaptive outdoor equipment designed for people with limited function.

"Dad, you're going to have to do things in a different way, but you don't have to give anything up," his son said.

It takes great perseverance to recover physically and emotionally from a paralyzing injury. For Drew, the source of his ability to persevere was the support of his wife, family, and friends—and of course, *his faith*.

"You maintain hope by having a belief in someone bigger and greater than yourself," Drew says. "If you don't have that or lose it, you end up in despair. That's the alternative. It's pretty black and white."

Drew saw evidence of this firsthand at Craig. One man in his early twenties named Daryl, for instance, had been even more severely injured than Drew in a car accident. Drew and Daryl talked often of their mutual faith as they endured the long process of rehabilitation, physical therapy, and classes at the hospital. Daryl completed his rehab, finished his undergraduate degree, and enrolled in Denver Seminary.

Another young man at Craig was paralyzed from the chest down after a vehicle accident in Montana. Drew says he was a strong, good-looking guy who suddenly didn't feel like a whole person any-more. When they talked about how to get on with life, Drew sensed the young man's despair. Less than a year after the man left Craig, he died of a drug overdose.

I don't know the details of this young man's story or his faith, yet I can't help thinking of Jesus' words after He healed a Samaritan of leprosy: "Rise and go; your faith has made you well" (Luke 17:19).

Drew's story is still being written. Four months after entering Craig Hospital, he completed his rehabilitation and was discharged. He came home to a house that family, friends, and neighbors had remodeled for a wheelchair-bound resident. Some of the same friends presented him with a new hand-cycle.

Today, Drew is back working full time as an attorney and providing for his family. Six months after leaving Craig, he joined the Bicycle Tour of Colorado and completed his first hundred-mile day as a hand-cyclist. In 2007 he finished second at the Off-Road Handcycling World Championships in Crested Butte, Colorado, and in 2009 he competed against some of the world's best in the Sadler's Alaska Challenge, the longest and toughest hand-cycle race on the planet. Drew has also returned to the slopes of Colorado on a mono-ski and celebrated his twenty-fifth wedding anniversary by scuba diving with his wife in the Caribbean.

"When things are good and your health is good, it's easy to think you're in control, that you're the one in charge," Drew says. "But when you wake up every day with a reminder that certain unex-pected events in life may leave you helpless and alone, even if you work hard and learn to overcome them, it's easier to depend on God.

It's a constant reminder that He is your salvation and you have a lot to be thankful for.

"When you have something that makes you helpless, you're drawn to what gives you strength."[3]

The Path to Godly Perseverance

We've said a great deal about perseverance in this chapter. But it's one thing to talk about it and quite another to put it into practice. When everything in your world seems to be falling apart, the idea of hanging on or even pushing forward can be more than daunting. You know you need God to make it, but you may wonder what that means in practical terms.

I think the path to godly perseverance begins with *prayer*.

Nothing connects us to heavenly power quite like regular discussion with our Maker. When you think about it, it's pretty incredible. We are able to have an ongoing conversation with the Creator of the universe at any time and at any place—no appointment needed! What's even more amazing is that He is always eager to hear from us. His desire for us is to "always pray and not give up" (Luke 18:1).

When prayer is a regular habit we're more likely to depend on Him for the solutions to our problems. Even though I know better, I still sometimes try to deal with issues and crises in my own strength. But sooner or later I remember what Jesus said to the disciples about prayer: "Ask and it will be given to you; seek and you will find; knock and the door will be opened to you. For everyone who asks receives; he who seeks finds; and to him who knocks, the door will be opened" (Luke 11:9–10).

That doesn't mean we'll always get exactly what we ask for. Sometimes God's plan is for us to simply endure for a little while (or a long while) longer. And if our request grows out of ungodly motives—selfishness or a desire for revenge, for example—we can be pretty sure we won't get the response we want. The Lord won't contradict Himself to answer our prayers.

For me, the model for taking troubles to God is Jesus' prayer in the garden at Gethsemane: "Father, if you are willing, take this cup from me; yet not my will, but yours be done" (Luke 22:42). I follow His example by asking for His strength. When the Lord is with me, I know I can handle anything.

Another great way to develop godly perseverance is to regularly read biblical accounts of those who have persisted in the midst of persecution or trouble. For example:

- Joseph persevered through terrible relationships with his brothers—through hate so intense that they nearly killed him before selling him into slavery. Then Joseph was imprisoned and forgotten by friends. Yet Joseph never turned his back on the Lord, and God stood by him. Two years after he was imprisoned, Joseph was promoted to second in command under Pharaoh, in charge of all of Egypt (Gen. 41:39–40). When his brothers came to him without recognizing him, Joseph didn't take revenge. He revealed himself to his brothers and treated them with kindness (Gen. 45).

- Centuries later, when Lazarus died, his sisters Martha and Mary both expressed great faith (John 11:21, 27, 32). Martha said to Jesus, "I know that even now God will give you whatever you ask" (v. 22). Their persevering faith led to what seemed impossible, and Lazarus was raised from the dead (vv. 43–44). Though Christ provided the power, He made it clear that the amazing faith of Martha and Mary was an essential part of the equation: "Did I not tell you that if you believed, you would see the glory of God?" (v. 40).

- Jesus Himself was the ultimate example of perseverance. Despite opposition from both the Jewish and Roman authorities, He continued to teach and speak on behalf of our Father in heaven before allowing Himself to be crucified as if He were a common criminal. When He made Himself human, there was a cost. Jesus felt the pain. He suffered as we suffer. Yet out of love for us, He persevered even to death. We should be encouraged that Scripture tells us the perseverance of Jesus is available to us as well: "May the Lord direct your hearts into God's love and Christ's perseverance" (2 Thess. 3:5).

In the eleventh chapter of Hebrews, we read about the persevering faith possessed by many of the Bible's greatest heroes, including those who

> faced jeers and flogging, while still others were chained and put in prison. They were stoned; they were sawed in two; they were put to death by the sword. They went about in sheepskins and goatskins, destitute, persecuted and mistreated—the world was not worthy of them. (Heb. 11:36–38)

After relating a long list of these saints and their commendable faith, the author of Hebrews advises us on how to achieve this unswerving faith: "Therefore, since we are surrounded by such a great cloud of witnesses, let us throw off everything that hinders and the sin that so easily entangles, and let us run with perseverance the race marked out for us" (12:1).

What does it mean to throw off everything that hinders us? I think it has to do with knowing what distracts us or detracts from our faith in the Lord. Maybe TV, movies, or the Internet distract us. Perhaps it's certain people in our lives who seem to lead us in directions we know we shouldn't go. Maybe it's the environment and culture that surrounds our job.

I believe a proactive approach is what's being called for here. It's pretty tough to persevere in our lives and faith if we use up our energy fighting unnecessary battles. When we go to the Lord in prayer, He'll help us identify where we need the most help and show us the next step. If we can learn to eliminate the distractions and traps that block us from connecting with God and His strength, we'll be ready to run with perseverance the race He has in mind for us.

The Promise

Many of us, when we first give our hearts to Jesus, are filled with love and enthusiasm for Him. Although we may be short on spiritual knowledge, we get excited about whatever the Lord might have for us next. At the outset, we are a bright light ready to shine on the world.

Our Enemy doesn't want to see us in this condition, of course. So he chips away at us. He engineers temptations to block our way and whispers lies into our ears. As the days grow into years, some of us weary of this battle. We begin to consider the temptations and listen to the lies. And we start to see our troubles as nothing more than a part of life to be endured.

This is the point when perseverance is most important. This, I believe, is when we must rely on God's power—*and remember His promise.*

Scripture addresses these moments:

> Remember those earlier days after you had received the light, when you stood your ground in a great contest in the face of suffering. Sometimes you were publicly exposed to insult and persecution; at other times you stood side by side with those who were so treated. You sympathized with those in prison and joyfully accepted the confiscation of your property, because you knew that you yourselves had better and lasting possessions.
>
> So do not throw away your confidence; it will be richly rewarded. You need to persevere so that when you have done the will of God, you will receive what he has promised. (Heb. 10:32–36)

What is the message here? The message is to remain faithful and confident! To remember that there is a purpose for our suffering. To realize that the Lord promised us a reward beyond what we can imagine.

Jesus makes a fascinating statement to the disciples that I believe speaks to this promise and reward. He says, "No one who has left home or brothers or sisters or mother or father or children or fields for me and the gospel will fail to receive a hundred times as much in this present age (homes, brothers, sisters, mothers, children and fields—and with them, persecutions) and in the age to come, eternal life" (Mark 10:29–30).

The reward in this life for our faith and perseverance is not financial. But it does promise to be rich in relationships with other believers. No doubt through those relationships, it promises to include places around the world where we can lay our heads at night. It also promises that we will see our "fields" increased a hundred times. I don't think this is a guarantee that we'll become wealthy land barons. I believe it's a statement that we'll see God's kingdom, which is also our kingdom, spread to new lands.

What's really interesting about this statement by Jesus, though, is what He says about persecution. He seems to indicate that if we persevere in faith, the level of persecution we encounter won't disappear; rather, *it will increase a hundredfold!* Even more interesting, Jesus seems to include these persecutions as part of our reward.

That doesn't make a lot of sense—unless we buy into the concept that suffering for Him is something to celebrate and that our trials are actually the foundation of our strength and hope.

That view puts persecution into an entirely new perspective.

Perhaps this starts to make more sense when we remember the final part of Jesus' statement that our reward, undoubtedly the best part, will also arrive in the "age to come" (v. 30). I wouldn't be surprised to learn that in heaven, we'll gather around the table (or maybe a campfire) and tell great tales of the glorious persecutions we experienced in our earthly life on behalf of the eternal kingdom of

God. Perhaps we'll sit amidst the heroes of the faith, including the martyrs of the first-century church. I wonder how it will feel to join in that company. What will those conversations be like?

My hope is that as you and I take our places in that mighty eternal throng, we'll be able to share our own stories of perseverance, of doing the right thing and sacrificing our lives for love, freedom, and truth. This is our future, our destiny.

Just thinking about that gets me excited. I can't imagine a greater reward—can you?

Chapter 9

Strength through Character

Sixteen-year-old Abby was the proud owner of a new driver's license. Now she wanted the chance to show off her skills. She pleaded with Lori, her mother, for a chance to drive. Lori saw an opportunity to fill two needs with one shopping trip. She handed her daughter a grocery list and a hundred-dollar bill and sent her off to Walmart with an admonition to "be careful."

Abby arrived safely at the store. She checked her hair and lipstick and sauntered in. With the grocery list and single bill in hand, she maneuvered through the aisles, filling her grocery cart as she walked.

Soon Abby finished her shopping and was ready to pay for her collection. But her sense of accomplishment suddenly turned to panic. The hundred-dollar bill—*where was it?* Abby searched her pockets. She retraced her steps through the store. The money was gone.

Abby's eyes filled with tears. She ran to the customer service counter and wailed, "I lost my mom's hundred-dollar bill! She sent me in for groceries, and I lost it! She is going to be so mad at me!"

The customer service employees took Abby's name and phone number. There was little else they could do. Most likely, Abby's terrible mistake had already made someone else's week.

When Abby told her mother what had happened, Lori was upset, but she didn't punish her daughter. Instead, they sat down together and prayed that the hundred dollars would be found and returned.

At 10:00 p.m., their phone rang. It was a Walmart employee. Incredibly, a college student had found the bill and turned it in. In a moment, one phone call transformed Abby's awful day. She and her mother were overjoyed.[1]

I don't know much about the student who returned Abby's money, but I can tell you that he or she is a person of character. The dictionary defines character as "moral excellence and firmness."[2] We might say that character is also embodied by honesty, honor, and integrity. However we define character, I'm sure we agree that the student who turned in the money at Walmart has it.

Thanks to our discussion in the last chapter, we can also agree that character is a product of perseverance: "Suffering produces perseverance; perseverance, character; and character, hope" (Rom. 5:3–4).

I don't know how that idea strikes you, but it sounds a little backward to me. I would expect that a person with character would find it easier to persevere through difficult circumstances. That makes sense. But how does perseverance produce character? When I look at the world around me, it seems to me that most things actually *decay* over time rather than grow stronger. The longer we live in our home, the more I see spots that need a paint touch-up. The longer I drive my car, the more I find I need to take it in for tune-ups and repairs. And the longer I live, the more I realize my body isn't what it used to be!

But maybe this process of perseverance leading to character works differently. Surely God is the X-factor. When you add God to the equation, persistence over time builds up character and strength instead of taking it away.

Consider, if you will, the snowball. Left by itself, it doesn't amount to much. It's just a little round chunk of white frozen water. Yet place that snowball at the top of a steep hill on a snowy day, and things begin to change. If you invest some time rolling that snowball across the ground so it picks up snow and grows into a larger ball, you begin to create something big and heavy. If you invest even more time and energy (this is where perseverance comes in), you might get that ball rolling down the hill. And the longer it rolls, the faster it goes, the bigger it gets.

Now you've got something powerful. This is a force to be reckoned with. This is when people start running for cover. Your little snowball suddenly becomes a runaway freight train!

I believe that equation of suffering, which produces perseverance, which produces character, works in a similar fashion. Our willingness to trust and rely on the Lord in a time of trouble invites His power to work in our lives. The more we trust and depend on Him, the easier it becomes. As the Lord says, "My yoke is easy and my burden is light" (Matt. 11:30).

Pretty soon our perseverance enables the Lord to add character to our "snowball"—and the more we persevere, the stronger we grow.

We find ourselves rolling downhill toward a godly life. It still might be a bumpy ride, but the size and momentum of our snowball just about guarantees that as long as we are pursuing God's will for our lives, nothing will stop us.

A Fateful Choice

Scripture makes it clear that character is important to God. David says, "I know, my God, that you test the heart and are pleased with integrity" (1 Chron. 29:17). James writes, "Who is wise and understanding among you? Let him show it by his good life, by deeds done in the humility that comes from wisdom" (James 3:13). And Paul writes, "Whatever happens, conduct yourselves in a manner worthy of the gospel of Christ" (Phil. 1:27).

Character is important to most of us, too. I'll never forget the day mine was called into question.

When I was in sixth grade, my homeroom teacher was a man I respected and admired. Mr. Fried was a reserve deputy sheriff for the city and taught karate. He projected a no-nonsense aura of power. He was everything I thought a man should be.

One day Mr. Fried asked his students to create a poster with an antidrug headline. I chose to draw a Formula One racing car and made up a slogan that I wrote above it: *Keep Speed on the Right Track*. I didn't remember where I'd learned that speed was a drug—probably from my older brothers and sisters.

After I turned in my poster, Mr. Freid asked me to stay after class. I figured he was going to tell me what a great job I'd done on my poster.

I was wrong.

"Jimmy, do you know what *plagiarism* is?" he asked.

"No," I said. "Should I?"

"Plagiarism is when you pass someone's idea off as your own. You *did* know that your slogan was supposed to be an original idea, right?"

I nodded. I didn't see where this was going.

"So," Mr. Fried continued, "where did you get yours from?"

Suddenly, I was crushed. Even when I explained to Mr. Fried that I must have heard about speed from my older siblings, he didn't believe me. Despite all the crazy things that happened to me during my childhood, the moment when Mr. Freid doubted my integrity was one of the most demoralizing of all. If he thought I was dishonest, he obviously didn't think much of me.

In many ways, our character defines us. Its value may seem obvious. What seems clear on paper, however, can get mighty foggy when we're challenged by real-life circumstances.

Author Tim Kimmel tells the story of a hunting trip he took with a friend named Tom. A successful businessman, Tom was a leader in his church, a family man, and a warm and friendly guy. During their trip into the mountains, however, Tim noticed that Tom was unusually quiet.

Around their campfire that first night, the story came out. Tom's high-school-age daughter was pregnant. Tom couldn't believe that all the spiritual training he'd offered over the years had been ignored or forgotten. The little girl he loved so much had made a fateful and life-altering choice.

Tim asked what they would do: *keep the baby or put it up for adoption?*

The answer shocked Tim to his toes.

"We considered the alternatives, Tim," this grieving father said, his eyes on the ground. "Weighed all the options. We finally made an appointment with the abortion clinic. I took her down there myself."

Tim dropped the stick he'd been holding. For years, Tom had been an outspoken opponent of abortion. He'd even served at a crisis pregnancy center in his city.

The conversation continued. "I know what I *believe*, Tim, but that's different than what I had to *do*. I had to make a decision that had the least amount of consequences for the people involved."

Tim sensed that his friend had rehearsed those lines. He later wrote, "By the look in his eyes and the emptiness in his voice, I could tell his words sounded as hollow to him as they did to me."[3]

Tom had somehow convinced himself that an abortion was the choice with the "least consequences." Worse, he had compromised his own beliefs and his character and, in the process, brought terrible new devastation upon his family and an unborn child.

The Integrity of the Upright

Based on Tim Kimmel's story, I have to conclude that Tom's character was superficial. It wasn't rooted in suffering and perseverance. It wasn't strong enough to help him make the wise and godly choice.

Genuine character points us toward an eternal path and protects us from trouble and tragedy: "The integrity of the upright guides them, but the unfaithful are destroyed by their duplicity" (Prov. 11:3).

In the early days of the church, a couple named Ananias and Sapphira apparently lacked this depth of integrity and character as well. The believers at that time shared everything, including the proceeds from the sale of land. When Ananias and Sapphira sold a piece of property, Ananias (with Sapphira's knowledge) kept some of the money for himself. He pretended to present the full proceeds of the sale to the apostles.

Somehow, Peter knew.

"What made you think of doing such a thing?" he said to Ananias. "You have not lied to men but to God." Upon hearing Peter's words, Ananias fell down and died on the spot. His body was wrapped up and carried away.

Three hours later, not knowing what had happened, Sapphira came to Peter. "Tell me," Peter said, "is this the price you and Ananias got for the land?"

"Yes," Sapphira answered, "that is the price."

"How could you agree to test the Spirit of the Lord?" Peter said. "Look! The feet of the men who buried your husband are at the door, and they will carry you out also."

Sapphira also fell down and died. She was buried next to Ananias (see Acts 5:1–10).

This is a pretty clear example of how highly the Lord values integrity and of the devastation that can destroy us if we don't cultivate character through perseverance. It's not something to mess around with. In one form or another, deception leads to death.

On the other hand, the practice of good and godly character—difficult as it may be at the time—moves us toward a future of promise.

Jonas Beiler is a man of character. The product of an old-order Amish family, he grew up in Lancaster County, Pennsylvania. His early trade was as an auto mechanic; he was always good at fixing things.

In 1968, he fixed his future on a pretty Amish girl named Anne. They were engaged in January and married in September. The first years of their marriage were happy ones and included the births of two daughters, LaWonna and Angie. But tragedy entered their lives in 1975. Anne's sister accidently backed over Angie, just nineteen months old, with a tractor. She was killed immediately.

Anne fell into depression. She began sleeping at night on the sofa, not wanting Jonas to know she cried herself to sleep. An emotional wall rose between them. Even so, Jonas did his best to encourage his wife.

For Jonas, the road got even tougher on a day in 1981. That's when Anne revealed a terrible secret. In the weeks following Angie's death, their pastor had taken advantage of Anne's emotional vulnerability. He'd manipulated her into an affair, one that had continued for most of the past six years.

"I'm sorry," Anne said. "And I'm a sorry person."

That night, Anne didn't know what her husband would do. Would he kick her out? Would he leave her? If he attacked her verbally, Anne didn't think she could take it. She would have to run away.

Instead, Jonas's words took her breath away.

"I want you to be happy …" he said. "Just promise me that you won't leave me in the middle of the night with a note on my dresser. If you decide to leave, just tell me about it. I'll help you pack. I just want you to promise you'll take the girls with you, because they need their mother."

Incredibly, Jonas told Anne that he wanted her to stay, that she was a good mother, that he was willing to forgive her. They were the words she needed to hear. They were the words of a man ready to stand by his wife, a man of godly character.

The story doesn't end there. A few years later, the Beilers purchased a food stand at a farmer's market in Pennsylvania. The menu included soft pretzels, though they weren't particularly good. When Jonas tried a new recipe for the pretzels, however, sales suddenly took off, and a booming business was born. Auntie Anne's Pretzels grew into the world's largest mall-based pretzel operation, with franchises and locations worldwide.

The success of Auntie Anne's enabled Jonas to fulfill a dream. In 1992, he established the Family Resource and Counseling Center, which today offers affordable, faith-based counseling to people in need. He is still finding ways to fix things.

Despite these achievements, Jonas's character was tested again. In 2003, Anne confessed to another affair, which had happened in the mid-nineties, in the midst of family struggles and business pressures.

Once again, Jonas didn't erupt with anger. He didn't boot Anne out of the house or ask for a divorce. Instead, he suggested they see a marriage counselor. At that first meeting with the counselor, Jonas told Anne he didn't want to leave, that he wanted to work with her on their relationship.[4]

In her autobiography *Twist of Faith,* Anne says of her husband,

> Jonas has been my rock and was the one person
> in my life who loved me unconditionally. He was
> the man who loved me in a way that all of us want

to be loved. Through all of my sin, despair, and
depression he stayed with me; and quietly, day in
and day out, year after year, he stayed committed
to our family.[5]

Jonas Beiler felt the pain of betrayal and the loss of a child, yet
his suffering produced perseverance, and his perseverance, character—not only in himself, but also in Anne. Who can say what
would have happened if Jonas had hardened his heart against his wife
and allowed their marriage to crumble? We do know that today the
Beilers are enjoying a restored marriage and the rewards of pursuing
Jonas's dream of counseling people in need. His strength of character
ultimately saved himself and his family from the devastation that
strikes so many today.

Setting an Example

When we seek to live lives of godly character, we benefit personally from the Lord's protection and guidance. But our strength of
character does more. It serves as an example and an encouragement
to our spouses, our children, our friends, and everyone with whom
we come into contact.

Back in the thirties and forties, there was a Swedish mother
raising nine children in Chicago. "Mumma" Lind often took her
children along to ride on the streetcar, a red-and-cream-colored trol-
ley. Sometimes the conductor let some of the kids ride for free even
though they were old enough to pay. The fare was only a few pennies,
but in those days, every cent was valuable. Mumma never objected to
the conductor's kindness.

Years later, however, Mumma Lind began to think about all those free rides. It was important to her that everything was right between her and *var Herre* (Swedish for "Our Lord"). Even though funds were still scarce, she decided to pay the money back. She sent a letter explaining the situation to the Chicago Transit Authority and included a ten-dollar bill, which at the time was enough money to feed her family for two weeks.

The transit authority responded with its own letter:

> Dear Mrs. Lind:
>
> We hereby acknowledge receipt of the $10.00 bill and extend to you our sincerest appreciation of your honesty and integrity.
>
> It is always gratifying to observe and to know of instances of personal action that follow the rules of Christian conduct.

For years, Mumma kept this letter in her Bible. Eventually it was accorded a place of honor on the wall in one of her daughter's homes.[6]

This seemingly insignificant gesture is a testament to the kind of character Mumma Lind possessed. You can bet that her kids took notice. One of her children, Lucille, later wrote about the incident in a book about her mother.

We don't always realize how often those around us, especially our children, watch and are influenced by every move we make. Even the smallest act of integrity can leave an impression that lasts generations. That's why Scripture advises us to be a model for the young: "In everything set them an example by doing what is good" (Titus 2:7). Like the transit authority employee, we appreciate and are encouraged by true integrity and character when we see it.

Character in Action

Our character is most influential when we have allowed suffering and perseverance to write it onto our hearts. I'm talking about a godly character so deeply ingrained that we don't even hesitate to put it into motion. It becomes part of who we are.

Todd Pierce is a man with this kind of character. You could say that Todd is a "cowboy's cowboy." For six years he was a professional bareback horseman competing in rodeos across the United States. Todd was one of the best—he was consistently ranked among the top twenty in the world.

But Todd's success in the arena came at a price. Nearly every year that he competed, he suffered a major injury. It started when a horse fell on top of him, causing a double fracture in his lower arm and leading to the insertion of a metal plate there. Once that injury healed and Todd was released to ride again, he broke the same arm in a different spot. Todd endured a year and a half of bone-graft operations and the painful reinsertion of the metal plate.

Then Todd broke a finger on his riding hand, which he broke two more times. That was followed by a knee injury, which included torn anterior and posterior cruciate ligaments.

The final blow occurred at the Calgary Stampede in 2000 when Todd reinjured the same knee. The subsequent surgery triggered the flare-up of a rare nerve disorder that eventually took him to the famous Mayo Clinic in Minnesota. When doctors told Todd he faced at least a year of recovery time, he knew it was time to hang up his competitive spurs.

Todd stood at a crossroads. Rodeo wasn't the most important thing in his life—God, his wife, and his family held that place. But his niche for serving the Lord had been sharing his faith with fellow riders on the rodeo circuit. What was he supposed to do now?

The answer began to materialize when Todd was asked to speak at a rodeo ministry event. One thing led to another; soon Todd was back in the saddle—not as a competitor, but as a pastor for the Professional Bull Riders organization.

The life of a bull rider is not only dangerous but also lonely and full of temptation. The season runs from January through November, so riders are on the road nearly all year. Young fans, many of them female, follow the riders from one venue to another as if they were rock stars. Most of Todd's ministry involves talking with the bull riders, sharing his faith, and encouraging them to persevere as husbands, fathers, and men of integrity.

Occasionally, however, Todd has the opportunity to serve in a more dramatic fashion.

One of those moments occurred in 2004 during the Anaheim Open in Southern California. Todd had just helped a veteran rider named B. J. Kramps as he mounted a bull in the bucking chute. As Todd prepared to help the next rider, he watched Kramps enter the arena.

As Todd and a capacity crowd looked on, the bull bucked Kramps off his right side. Kramps tried to get up and scramble away, but the rope tied around the bull's belly had rolled over his hand. Kramps was caught.

Todd held his breath when the bull, instead of staying close and bucking, took off running across the arena, dragging Kramps with him. Three bullfighters—the bull-riding equivalent of rodeo clowns, men charged with protecting fallen riders—desperately gave chase.

At the far end of the arena, the bull turned and, outrunning the bullfighters, charged back toward where Todd sat. The bull reached the end of the arena at Todd's left and rumbled toward the bucking chute.

Todd's gut tightened. Kramps, still being dragged and stepped on by the bull, appeared unconscious.

Oh my gosh, Todd thought. *B. J.'s gettin' killed.*

When the fifteen-hundred-pound bull roared past the bucking chute, Todd didn't stop to consider the risk or the potential for aggravating his past injuries. He leaped from the six-foot fence over the back of the bull, trying to grab the rope that ensnared Kramps.

He missed and fell into the dirt.

The bull stopped at the arena's right corner just twenty feet away, turned, and charged Todd.

Todd scrambled to his feet. He and the bull were eye to eye. At the last moment, Todd jumped onto the bull's head, shooting to miss the pair of deadly horns and grab the rope at the same time.

This time Todd succeeded. At the same moment, one of the bullfighters also got hold of the rope. Together, they freed Kramps.

Todd smothered Kramps with his body to protect him from further injury while the bullfighters distracted the bull. Soon the danger was past.

Todd looked down at Kramps, fearing the worst. Kramps opened his eyes. With typical cowboy deadpan, he said, "You can get off me now."

B. J. Kramps recovered from the incident with no lasting effects. So did Todd—with the exception of a thousand-dollar fine for unauthorized entry into the arena. Yet his quick and heroic action won the appreciation of Kramps and everyone in attendance that day.

Todd's reasoning for what he did was simple: "When you're filled with the love of God, your knee-jerk reaction is to go to someone's aid. When you're compelled to love, you just do it."[7]

I think Todd's attitude explains the quick action of a military veteran I learned of recently. During the Vietnam War, a hand grenade was lobbed into his company of soldiers. This brave soldier didn't run, didn't calculate his chances of survival, and didn't hesitate to act. Instead, he immediately threw himself down on the grenade to protect his buddies. He was willing to die if necessary so that his fellow soldiers could live.

The brave soldier was injured, but he lived.

We can find character in action on rodeo grounds and on the battlefield. We'll also find it in our families.

On my blog, I recently wrote about a father who was walking down a city street to a McDonald's with his four-year-old daughter. This father noticed that a car coming their way was moving erratically. The vehicle suddenly roared in their direction—and there was no time to escape. The surrounding buildings were built nearly on top of the sidewalks, so there was nowhere to run. Just before impact, the father grabbed his daughter and held her above his head.

She lived. He died.

I'm sure she'll never forget his sacrifice.

God's love inside us, refined by suffering and perseverance, produces a condition that doesn't require any investigation or risk analysis. It translates into immediate, life-giving action. When you're compelled to love, you just do it.

That is character.

Live Such Good Lives

Character is holy. It is powerful. It changes lives and history. When we demonstrate a deep-rooted, faith-based character, it could even be described as a form of worship. This is one of the primary ways we bring glory to the Lord and inspire others to do the same.

The apostle Peter wrote to the members of the early Christian church, "You are a chosen people, a royal priesthood, a holy nation, a people belonging to God, that you may declare the praises of him who called you out of darkness into his wonderful light" (1 Peter 2:9).

But Peter does not stop there. He goes on to explain *how* we are to declare the Lord's praises: "Dear friends, I urge you, as aliens and strangers in the world, to abstain from sinful desires, which war against your soul. Live such good lives among the pagans that, though they may accuse you of doing wrong, they may see your good deeds and glorify God on the day he visits us" (vv. 11–12).

Our good lives and good deeds—our demonstrations of godly character—help us to resist our sinful desires and move others toward salvation. When we unleash strong character through our actions, we deliver glory to the kingdom of heaven.

Consider the story of Ellie, a Jewish teenager held in a German concentration camp during World War II. After months of malnutrition,

Ellie realized her only chance to survive was escape. If she didn't act quickly, she would die of starvation.

One night, after much careful planning, Ellie made her move. She had climbed halfway up the barbed wire fence that surrounded the camp, nearly free, when an armed SS guard screamed at her to stop.

Ellie dropped to the ground, beaten. She sobbed, aware that her life was now over.

Suddenly the guard spoke in an astonished voice: "Ellie? Is that you? It can't be possible!"

Ellie looked up and recognized the face staring back at her. It was Rolf, the boy who had been her best friend in middle school.

"Oh, Rolf, go ahead and kill me. Please! I have no reason to live. I have lost all hope. Get it over with, and let me die now. There's nothing to live for anyway."

"Ellie, you are so wrong. There is everything to live for so long as you know *who* to live for. I'm going to let you go. I'll guard you until you climb the wall and get on the other side. But would you promise me one thing?"

By the intensity on Rolf's face, Ellie knew he wasn't joking. "What is it, Rolf?"

"Promise me that when you get on the other side and become free, that you will ask one question continuously until someone answers it for you. Ask, 'Why does Jesus Christ make life worth living?' Promise me, Ellie! He's the only reason to live. Promise me you'll ask until you get the answer."

"Yes, I promise, I promise!" Ellie said.

Ellie scrambled back up the fence. As she dropped to the other side, she heard gunshots. Her first thought was that Rolf had changed his mind. But when she looked, she was horrified to discover that other guards had seen Rolf allow her to escape and killed him immediately.

Ellie ran to freedom. As she ran, she realized that the single reason her friend had died was so that she could know this Jesus.[8]

Though I don't know Rolf's background, I can guess that he had seen and known suffering. Clearly, despite the awful circumstances surrounding him, he had persevered in his faith. When the moment arrived for his character to shine through, he didn't hesitate. It cost him his earthly life—and earned him a place of honor for eternity.

Suffering … perseverance … character. What do these add up to?

Hope.

Let's talk about that.

Chapter 10

Strength through Hope

There is incredible power in hope.

A woman once suffered with bleeding for twelve years, perhaps from a menstrual disorder. In an attempt to gain relief, this woman spent her life's savings on doctors. The doctors failed to cure her condition, however. In fact, their efforts *increased* her suffering. To make matters worse, according to the custom of that time, a bleeding woman was considered "unclean." Therefore, she wasn't allowed to touch or be touched by anyone.

Think about this for a moment. You're a woman who's been dealing with bleeding, pain, and weakness for *twelve years.* Your financial resources are gone. In all that time, you haven't been able to receive the encouragement of even a simple hug.

That's a pretty grim situation. Many people, if not most, would give up under those circumstances. They would let go of any thoughts about a better future. They would fold up their dreams and throw them away.

Yet this woman didn't do that. When she heard about a teacher who was drawing large crowds, performing miracles, and talking about God, she went to this teacher. He was on the move when she arrived and surrounded by followers. Yet she pressed in. She desperately wanted to touch the teacher's cloak.

You see, despite all the years of pain and misery, she still held out hope for healing, for a different life. She realized that this man, the one they called Jesus, was unlike any "cure" she'd encountered before. He was *the* answer. She believed that a single touch was all she needed.

You know the rest of the story. From behind Him, the woman touched Jesus' garment. Immediately, she knew that she was healed. Jesus turned around and asked who had touched His clothes. The woman, now trembling because her action had rendered Jesus ceremonially unclean, explained her behavior.

"Daughter, your faith has healed you," Jesus told her. "Go in peace and be freed from your suffering" (Mark 5:34).

This long-suffering woman easily could have stayed home the day Jesus walked through her town. She could have missed the opportunity that changed everything. But her newly acquired faith, born of a long-nurtured hope, gave her freedom for eternity.

Hope is powerful. It is our reason to get up in the morning no matter how terrible the day before. It is the weapon that can outlast any enemy. Hope is what gives our life meaning.

The most powerful hope of all is the kind we've been talking about in the last two chapters, the type that Paul first explained to believers in Rome. Let's look at Paul's words again:

> We rejoice in the hope of the glory of God. Not
> only so, but we rejoice in our sufferings, because we

> know that suffering produces perseverance; perse-
> verance, character; and character, hope. And hope
> does not disappoint us, because God has poured
> out his love into our hearts by the Holy Spirit,
> whom he has given us.
>
> You see, at just the right time, when we were
> still powerless, Christ died for the ungodly.... God
> demonstrates his own love for us in this: While we
> were still sinners, Christ died for us. (Rom. 5:2–6, 8)

Suffering leads to perseverance. Perseverance produces character. Character delivers hope—and not just any hope, but a hope that does not disappoint, a hope infused with God's love. *Powerful* hope.

Did you catch this phrase: "When we were still powerless, Christ died for the ungodly" (v. 6)? Paul implies here that we had no power before Jesus. But thanks to His death and the hope released on the cross, we now possess the greatest power available to humanity.

This is a hope strong enough to heal and bring peace to a bleeding woman after twelve years. It's a hope strong enough for you, too.

The Many Sides of Hope

Let's explore further what it means to acquire the hope of Christ. There are many sides to this hope, and Scripture gives us a picture of each of the facets and what these can mean for our lives.

Anchoring Hope

When the clouds darken, the seas begin to chop, and a storm suddenly descends on a ship at anchor, the well-being of cargo and crew depends not on good wishes but upon the chain and moorings of the anchor. In a similar way, if our hope is placed in the Lord, we know that it's more than a wish or a fantasy. We can be encouraged even in troubled times because, as the author of Hebrews said, "We have this hope as an anchor for the soul, firm and secure" (Heb. 6:19). Our souls are safely held in place by our Father in heaven no matter the outcome of our circumstances.

Patient Hope

God's plans for us are rarely understood ahead of the fact. So often, we are called on to trust and carry on. Anyone who has suffered and persevered knows what it means to wait for the Lord to act. It's not easy when everything seems to be falling apart around us. Our hope is often the key to finding the strength to keep going. This might be what the author of Lamentations had in mind when he wrote, "Yet this I call to mind and therefore I have hope: … 'The LORD is my portion; therefore I will wait for him'" (Lam. 3:21, 24).

Joyful Hope

It's hard to stay downcast if we truly believe in the glorious future that God has prepared for us—perhaps in this life, and most certainly in eternity. Again, I'm not talking about happiness that derives from temporary pleasures. I'm speaking of the deep and abiding joy that Jesus offers to each of us. Paul wrote, "Never be lacking in zeal, but keep your spiritual fervor, serving the Lord. Be joyful in hope" (Rom. 12:11–12). Let's focus on that joyful hope! A glorious future for each of us is so much closer than it appears.

Bold Hope

Part of the spiritual strength that we derive from hope is a commitment to be daring, and even audacious, in our faith. Peter, the same man who denied Jesus three times, showed us the way by his bold actions after the resurrection. He was instrumental in the formation of the early church, and he preached to thousands, performed miracles, was arrested, defied the Sanhedrin (the Jewish legal authority), and ultimately gave his life for his Lord. This most human and fallible of apostles is the perfect example of what we can become after gaining the power of hope in Christ: "Since we have such a hope, we are very bold" (2 Cor. 3:12).

Purifying Hope

Temptation is everywhere in this life—on the television, on the Internet, in the refrigerator, and on the sidewalks of most cities around the world. Yet our hope in the Lord gives us the strength to turn away from sin. Scripture says, "Now we are children of God, and what we will be has not yet been made known. But we know that when he appears, we shall be like him, for we shall see him as he is. Everyone who has this hope in him purifies himself, just as he is pure" (1 John 3:2–3). Suffering, perseverance, and character all help build a wall that stands between us and wrong thinking and wrongdoing. The more we embrace this kind of strong hope, the closer we move toward the purity of Christ.

Saving Hope

Diane Fassel was twenty-two years old and single when she discovered she was pregnant. The staff at the abortion clinic told her that what she carried inside of her was nothing more than a glob of cells and tissues. Immediately after the procedure, however, Diane realized that it was so much more. She was plagued by guilt over the abortion. She drank and partied, attempting to block out the pain she felt. Finally, she attempted to take her own life and failed. Then she saw a television show that talked about a God who was much different from the one she'd learned about growing up, one who was loving and forgiving. For the first time in months, she felt a trace of hope. Eventually, at the age of twenty-six, Diane gave her life to Christ.[1] Now she isn't trying to run from pain. She's at peace, living daily with the Lord's saving hope: "Let us be self-controlled, putting on faith and love as a breastplate, and the hope of salvation as a helmet" (1 Thess. 5:8).

Living Hope

Peter wrote, "In his great mercy he has given us new birth into a living hope through the resurrection of Jesus Christ from the dead" (1 Peter 1:3). The foundation of our hope is the resurrection of the living Christ. All of Christianity stands on the amazing truth that Jesus died on the cross yet rose on the third day, appearing to the apostles over a period of forty days (Acts 1:3) and to more than five hundred believers on one occasion (1 Cor. 15:6). Christ did the impossible—He conquered death. Because Jesus is alive today, because we can have a relationship with the living God right now, we *always* have hope.

Blessed Hope

As much as the Lord has given us through His love, grace, mercy, and power, we can hope for something more—the return of Christ to this world. Imagine not seeing a beloved son, daughter, or friend for many years, and then finding out that person will visit soon. Won't you wake up each morning filled with anticipation? Won't you count the days until his or her arrival and dream of what those first moments will be like? Won't your eagerness to be reunited define your hope for the future? That's a taste of the blessed hope described by Paul that is available to each of us:

> For the grace of God that brings salvation has appeared to all men. It teaches us to say 'No' to ungodliness and worldly passions, and to live self-controlled, upright and godly lives in this present age, while we wait for the blessed hope—the glorious appearing of our great God and Savior, Jesus Christ. (Titus 2:11–13)

Hope in a Mighty God

As men and women of faith, the strength of our hope is directly proportional to our belief in God's power and influence. If we believe in a small God, one who is perhaps benevolent but has little ability to sway the events of our lives, we possess a small hope. We don't have much to rely on when we're stuck in the crucible of a crisis. We hope, but we lack vision and confidence. Our prayers will fall short of what the Lord would have us ask for. We tend to put God in a box.

On the other hand, if we believe in a big God, one who is mighty enough to create the universe and every living creature in it, who is still actively making miracles and involved in our lives today, we possess a powerful hope. No matter how traumatic or tragic our circumstances, we know that anything is possible if it's in His will. We ask for the Lord's intervention in the great and minute issues of our lives, understanding that His power is unlimited.

We can learn something about hope and God's power by examining Psalm 147. We read about His supremacy in passages such as these: "He determines the number of stars and calls them each by name. Great is our Lord and mighty in power" (vv. 4–5) and "He sends his command to the earth; his word runs swiftly. He spreads the snow like wool and scatters the frost like ashes. He hurls down his hail like pebbles. Who can withstand his icy blast?" (vv. 15–17).

We also read about our relationship to God's power: "The LORD delights in those who fear him, who put their hope in his unfailing love" (v. 11). At first glance, it may seem odd that God prefers we both fear Him and hope in Him. That's why I like John Piper's perspective on this verse.

In his book *The Pleasures of God*, Piper invites his reader to imagine exploring a glacier in Greenland. As you arrive at the top of a steep cliff with an incredible view, a terrifying storm suddenly descends on you. When gusts threaten to blow you off the cliff, you fear for your life. But as you look for cover, you discover a cleft in the ice with just enough room for you. Here you wait out the storm, secure yet still trembling from the awesome force that surrounds you.

Piper compares this experience to how we are to view the mightiness of the Lord:

> In other words, God's greatness is greater than
> the universe of stars, and his power is behind the

unendurable cold of arctic storms. Yet he cups his hand around us and says, "Take refuge in my love and let the terrors of my power become the awesome fireworks of your happy night-sky." The fear of God is what is left of the storm when you have a safe place to watch right in the middle of it. And in that place of refuge we say, "This is amazing, this is terrible, this is incredible power; Oh, the thrill of being here in the center of the awful power of God, yet protected by God himself! Oh, what a terrible thing to fall into the hands of the living God without hope, without a Savior! Better to have a millstone tied around my neck and be thrown into the depths of the sea than to offend against this God! What a wonderful privilege to know the favor of this God in the midst of his power!"[2]

As believers, we have a front-row seat in the middle of the greatest storm in the universe. That is both exciting and more than a little scary. Yet even as we shiver in fear, we can claim the most amazing peace and hope. We are children of the living God. We have access to the mightiest power that exists.

Holy Confidence

Naive hope is based on wishful thinking, but a hope formed from suffering, perseverance, and character and rooted in faith in God is something else entirely. It is realistic, motivating, and awesome. It helps us see beyond the misery of the immediate to the possible. It is founded on the certainty of the Lord's love and power.

You might call this kind of hope a holy confidence. It's something I had only begun to develop after I invited Christ into my life in high school. It started to grow on the night that a football teammate of mine, Mike Nelson, invited me and a couple other guys to join him and his parents at a place called The Castle, which was a Victorian house converted into a concert venue.

The performers on this particular night were four guys with amazing singing voices. They sang contemporary songs, only they changed all the lyrics to represent Christian themes. These guys were good, especially the lead singer, and their music made a big impression on me.

After the concert, I went up to talk with the lead singer. He spent quite a few minutes with me, asking questions and praying. When he put his hand behind my neck to draw me in closer, I just lost it, and the tears began to flow. I talked about not having a mother or father. He told me that he didn't have a dad either, that he'd made bad choices and spent time in prison, but that he'd given his life to the Lord while incarcerated, a decision that had turned his life around.

That night filled me with hope. I knew that the Lord was on my side too. I woke up the next day with the same problems and questions about my future as before, yet I had a new sense of joy and confidence about what was ahead.

In my senior year, I continued to learn about the Lord and what it meant to hope in Him. Unfortunately, I started to develop a bit of an arrogant attitude—not about my faith, but about my football ability. I was our team's starting quarterback, and I received letter of intent offers from several big-time college programs. I thought I was pretty special. I even dreamed about a future in the NFL.

My brother Mike, who played college ball for the University of Nevada at Reno, came to watch me play one weekend. He liked what he saw on the field but was not impressed by what he saw off it.

"Jim, you know what?" he said. "You're getting a big head about playing football. You're not the same guy you used to be."

Fortunately, my faith was strong enough at this point that I didn't just blow off Mike's comments. Instead, I prayed about them. "Lord, what does this mean?" I asked. "Has football become an obsession? Should I give it up?" I didn't want to have a big ego, but I loved playing and being part of the team.

To my amazement, I sensed the Lord responding to my prayer, telling me that I was going in an unhealthy direction. Still, I wasn't sure. Did God really want me to give up football?

I still sought an answer when the time came to play our first league game. I decided to make an unusual and very specific request: "Lord," I prayed, "if You don't want me to play big-time college football, break a bone today ... but please don't let it hurt." Maybe it was a strange thing to ask for, but I really wanted to find an answer— preferably without too much pain in the process.

In the third quarter of that game, one of our running backs got ejected for throwing a punch. It was the only time during my high school career that one of my teammates was taken out of a game by a referee. His replacement was a wide-eyed sophomore.

On the first play after the ejection, I dropped back and looked for a receiver to pass to. From the corner of my eye, I saw the other team's outside linebacker rushing toward me at full speed. Our new running back, who was in the backfield to block, moved out of this guy's way to avoid contact. He never even touched the blitzing linebacker.

The guy leveled me.

When I got up from the turf, I noticed something wrong with my left arm. It didn't hurt, but I felt a pressure in my shoulder. I reached under my shoulder pad and felt the points of bones pushing up under my skin.

My collarbone was broken. I decided right then that my competitive football days were over. God had answered my prayer and, by doing so, gave me even greater confidence in Him and His wisdom for my future.

By the time I was a senior at Cal State San Bernardino, my hope and confidence in the Lord had grown. My holy confidence was put to an unexpected test on a highway near Big Bear Lake, California. My friend and roommate—I'll call him Phil—and I had just applied together for jobs at a ski resort. Since I had learned Japanese, I figured I could be a ski instructor to the resort's Japanese tourists. Phil was an EMT, so he thought he'd be valuable to the ski patrol.

We were driving home from the resort and talking about the possibilities. Our interviews had seemed to go well. If we got the jobs, we could rent a cabin for the winter. It was a perfect setup for a couple of college guys—good pay, great skiing, and a chance to meet "snow bunnies."

When we arrived back at our apartment, our answering machine gave us the good news. We were hired!

Yet as Phil and I talked about next steps, a "voice" began whispering to me. I sensed the Lord saying, *This is not going to be a good environment for you. If you do this, it will take you away from Me.*

I thought about my crazy life up to that point and how so much had changed since I'd given my heart to the Lord—my circumstances, sure, but even more: my faith, attitude, and hope in an eternal future. I didn't want to do anything to jeopardize my relationship with Him. I realized I now had confidence in Him and the direction He led.

Reluctantly, I turned to Phil and said, "You know, I think I'm going to have to call back and quit before I even start."

"What?" Phil said. "What about our cabin?"

I explained it to Phil. He was a Christian too, but he had a hard time understanding my decision. Nevertheless, I'd made up my mind. "I'm sorry, Phil," I said. "I just can't do it."

Even though I was nervous, I called the ski resort supervisor back and told him I'd changed my mind. I hated disappointing Phil and the supervisor, but going against the Lord would have been far worse. Phil, meanwhile, stayed with the ski patrol job.

About ten years later, I went to see Phil and caught up with him over lunch. He was a firefighter in Southern California and doing well in his career. After our lunch I asked, "How are you doing in your faith?"

"You know," he said, "I never really got that back on track after I took the ski patrol job."

I've lost touch with Phil, but my prayer for him is that he's regained his spiritual footing and reconnected to the hope found in Christ.

I don't share these examples from my life because I'm a great model of godly obedience. I've blown it plenty of times. But I do feel I've experienced moments in which the Lord used my suffering, perseverance, and character to build up my holy confidence and a hope that made me wiser and stronger—as long as I remember to listen to Him! That hope is available to all of us if we allow the Lord to do His work in our lives and spirits.

In my experience, these moments often came at key decision points in my life—what I would call forks in the road. In these times, it is as if the Lord says to me, "Choose a direction." There's no sense of judgment about which path I select. It feels more like a father wanting the best for his son. I have no doubt that He wants the best for you as well.

Let's talk more about hope by examining the example of three men who possessed an abundance of holy confidence.

Three Men and a Furnace

Roughly six centuries before the birth of Christ, King Nebuchadnezzar of Babylon and his armies besieged and conquered Jerusalem and its king. Four men of Judah—Daniel, Hananiah, Mishael, and Azariah, renamed Belteshazzar, Shadrach, Meshach, and Abednego—were subsequently chosen to serve the Babylonian king.

Thanks to Daniel's gift of prophecy and influence, Shadrach, Meshach, and Abednego were appointed as administrators in Babylon. Sometime after this, Nebuchadnezzar erected a statue of gold. You couldn't miss it—the statue stood ninety feet tall and nine feet wide.

The king then issued a command: Whenever music played, everyone in the kingdom had to bow down and worship the golden image. Anyone who didn't would be thrown into a blazing furnace.

After that declaration, naturally, everyone bowed down in the direction of the statue when the music started—everyone, that is, except Shadrach, Meshach, and Abednego. When some astrologers pointed this out to Nebuchadnezzar, he was furious. He summoned the trio and demanded obedience.

The king said, "Now when you hear the sound of the horn, flute, zither, lyre, harp, pipes and all kinds of music, if you are ready to fall down and worship the image I made, very good. But if you do not worship it, you will be thrown immediately into a blazing furnace. Then what god will be able to rescue you from my hand?" (Dan. 3:15).

The three men answered,

> O Nebuchadnezzar, we do not need to defend
> ourselves before you in this matter. If we are thrown
> into the blazing furnace, the God we serve is able
> to save us from it, and he will rescue us from your
> hand, O king. But even if he does not, we want you
> to know, O king, that we will not serve your gods
> or worship the image of gold you have set up. (vv.
> 16–18)

I love this response! The powerful king with his ego couldn't intimidate Shadrach, Meshach, and Abednego. They had a deep and abiding confidence in their God and His power, a firm hope that He would honor their courage and devotion. And yet … they left room for the Lord's will to be done. The depth of their faith was revealed in the words "even if he does not." They essentially said, "Even if God chooses not to save us, He knows best. We'll do the right thing and trust Him either way."

Shadrach, Meshach, and Abednego didn't try to put God in a corner. They didn't whisper a quick prayer to the effect of, "Okay, Lord, we're taking a stand here for You, so You'd better come through." They put their complete hope in Him and held on to their fear of a God who will not be manipulated. They left themselves wide open to the Lord's will. They knew they just needed to remain faithful to Him.

These three men had seen much in life. They'd had their lives turned upside down by a conquering army. The new regime forced them to move from their homeland and serve a king they neither respected nor admired. I think each of them had been through his share of suffering. They'd developed perseverance and character. And out of that experience, they discovered a powerful hope in the one true God.

That is holy confidence.

We know, of course, that God spared the lives of Shadrach, Meshach, and Abednego. Nebuchadnezzar grew so angry he had his furnace turned up seven times hotter than usual. It didn't matter. After the three were thrown in the furnace, the king reported seeing "four men walking around in the fire, unbound and unharmed, and the fourth looks like a son of the gods" (Dan. 3:25).

Nebuchadnezzar called Shadrach, Meshach, and Abednego out, and the king and his advisers saw that none of them was even singed. Nebuchadnezzar praised the God of these men who sent an angel to rescue His servants, and he decreed that anyone who said anything against their God be cut to pieces.

It doesn't always work this way, though, does it? Sometimes when believers put their complete hope in God, they still lose their earthly lives. This has been the fate of every martyr who died for faith throughout history.

Shadrach, Meshach, and Abednego knew this. That's why they used the words "even if he does not." Their hope wasn't based on present circumstances or what happened in the furnace. Essentially, it didn't matter whether they were rescued or not. They had a holy confidence founded on eternity and trust in the wisdom of a loving and all-knowing God.

Hope in His Plans and Power

The ultimate example of hope and trust, of course, is found in Jesus. When He stood before Pilate, Jesus refused to answer to any of the false accusations made by members of the Sanhedrin. This stunned Pilate because according to Roman law, silence by the accused required the Sanhedrin to make a pronouncement of guilt.

Jesus knew what His silence meant—flogging, mocking, the long march to Golgotha, and the slow and painful death on the cross. Yet as He stood before Pilate, He had great hope. It was not the hope of escape from the torment to come. It was a serene and holy confidence in the plans and power of our heavenly Father.

"For this reason I was born," Jesus told Pilate, "and for this I came into the world, to testify to the truth" (John 18:37).

When Pilate asked Jesus where He came from and Jesus said nothing, Pilate said, "Do you refuse to speak to me?… Don't you realize I have power either to free you or to crucify you?" (19:9–10).

Jesus then answered, "You would have no power over me if it were not given to you from above" (v. 11). He knew the source of all power. This knowledge gave Him the peace and strength to face the most unbearable circumstances, including His own death.

How do we face unbearable circumstances? Do we remember who holds the power? Do we trust God enough to say, "He will save me—and even if He does not, I will still hope in Him"?

This is hope that looks forward to the glory of God. It is hope that will never be disappointed. It's hope that rises out of suffering, perseverance, and character.

It is a powerful hope—*a hope you can count on for eternity.*

Chapter 11

A Vision of Strength

Bob Glaus understands the power of godly strength.

Bob, an associate with a construction company in Southern California, was a loving husband and father of two active children, five-year-old Alese and two-year-old Wesley. Bob rose before four each morning and padded into the family prayer room—really a den furnished with a rattan chair and sofa bed—to spend time in quiet conversation with the Lord. In the evening, he read his Bible, seeking to draw closer to God through His Word.

He'd been going through the book of Job. It struck him as a challenge from the Lord to any man or woman of faith: *How much do you love Me? Do you love Me only when things are great or also when times are tough?*

Bob thought about what this meant for him. If he lost his job and couldn't find another, would he be as strong and faithful as Job, or would he curse God? What if he got news from the doctor that he had just six months to live? What if his wife, Jan, and the kids were killed in a car accident?

Bob meditated on this thought and prayed about it. "Lord," he said, "certainly if those things happened, especially if I lost my family, it would be incredibly painful. But even so, I don't think I would deny You." It was a satisfying realization. It was also a time when Bob felt a strong affirmation of the Lord's presence.

On a Monday soon after this prayer, Bob got up for his usual time with the Lord. As he knelt next to the sofa to pray, he thought about a friend's baby who suffered from life-threatening convulsions. With his eyes closed, he raised his hands as if presenting the infant to God. At that moment, a strange vision began to flood Bob's mind. He saw his hands lifting a baby wrapped in white cloth toward a radiant blue sky. Suddenly the baby left Bob's hands and gently floated toward heaven.

"Lord, You can't take this baby," Bob said in the vision. "It has its whole life in front of it. God, You can't possibly take this baby." The baby kept rising higher in the sky. Bob was overwhelmed with emotion. He began to cry.

The vision changed. The scene in Bob's mind was of a series of steps that led down to a group of children playing. A little girl sat on a tricycle, and some boys played with a train set. Everyone was having a good time.

"Okay, Lord, I understand," Bob said in the vision. "Children in heaven are happy. I can see it. But what about their parents? How can they possibly live through this?"

As if a movie camera was panning to the left, the scene in Bob's mind shifted. He saw crutches, wheelchairs, gurneys, and stainless steel medical paraphernalia lying in a pile.

"Okay, Lord," Bob said. "I understand this, too. While on earth, these children were in wheelchairs and on crutches, and now they're not. They experienced pain and suffering, and now they don't. But what about the parents?"

The vision changed a final time. Bob looked over from behind the right shoulder of a person dressed in a white, shining robe. Cradled in this person's left arm was a smiling, cooing baby. Bob perceived that the person holding the baby was Jesus.

"Lord, I understand," Bob said again. "The baby is in heaven, and the baby is happy. *But what about the parents? How could they ever go through this?*"

For the first time, Bob heard a voice in his vision. "Bob," the voice said, "we love the children here too."

Suddenly, the vision ended. Bob lay back on the floor next to the couch. His face was wet with tears.

What was that about? he wondered. He'd never experienced anything like it. Bob wrote down his memories of the vision and tucked them into a desk drawer. *Maybe someday,* he thought, *Jan and I are going to meet some parents who lost a child, and I'll be able to tell them, "Don't worry. Children in heaven are happy."*

Later, however, Bob had a more sobering thought. He wondered if God was preparing him for a personal trial. The more he considered it, the more he thought he was right—and the more he prayed about it. "Lord," he said more than once, on his knees with his face to the floor, "all I ask is that when it comes, that I may be found faithful."[1]

God Gets to Be God

It is rare for someone to live like Forrest Gump—that is, a life that seems to go well at every turn. Most of us will experience challenges and tough times in our future. The Lord is preparing us for them today. We've seen in this book how God continually points us toward the broken road and how, like the potter at his spinning wheel, He takes the shattered pieces of our lives and shapes them into something stronger, more useful, and more beautiful than before.

We've also talked about how the trials we face can be the beginning of a progression to holy confidence and hope—not just any hope, but the firm conviction that we are where we need to be, that as believers our future rests in the firm hands of a sovereign God.

Most of us would never choose to go through hardship and tragedy. Yet it seems clear that this is part of God's design for His children. It seems like we *need* trials in order for Him to mold us and move us toward our destiny.

I think we can know that our relationship with the Lord is on the right track, that we are gaining in godly strength, when we can pray as Bob Glaus did, "Lord, all I ask is that when it comes, that I may be found faithful."

For Bob, "it" arrived about a year and a half after his vision. The Glaus family was on vacation, visiting friends in Oregon. Wesley, now four years old and a whirling dervish of energy, seemed pale and had recently suffered a nosebleed. Jan decided to take Wes to a doctor to check things out while Bob inspected a building project for the pastor of friends.

A few hours later, Bob was on his knees looking over an electrical connection when the pastor approached him.

"Bob, I have bad news," the pastor said. "Wesley has leukemia."

Bob was thankful he was already on his knees. He could barely take in the words.

Lord, I knew it was going to be bad, he prayed. *But I never thought it would be this bad.*

The tests showed that Wes had acute lymphoblastic leukemia, a potentially deadly cancer of the white blood cells. He needed to begin chemotherapy treatments immediately.

A friend said, "Bob, we're going to pray, and God is going to heal Wes."

Bob and Jan believed completely in the Lord's power to heal. But they had also joined with others in praying for the healing of a friend with multiple sclerosis and of a boy they knew who had a brain tumor.

Both the friend and the boy died.

Bob knew that not everyone is healed. As he put it, "God gets to be God." He told the friend, "God may heal Wesley or God may take Wesley home. But I know that whatever He decides to do will be the best for Jan, Alese, Wesley, and me."

The Lord expects us to ask for His favor and intervention, but we can get into trouble when we make demands of Him. According to Scripture, the children of Israel "willfully put God to the test by demanding the food they craved. They spoke against God, saying, 'Can God spread a table in the desert? When he struck the rock, water gushed out, and streams flowed abundantly. But can he also give us food?'" (Ps. 78:18–20).

Their demands ignited the Lord's anger. He gave the people what they asked for and more: manna, grain, and bread. He "rained meat down on them like dust, flying birds like sand on the seashore…. They ate till they had more than enough" (vv. 27, 29).

But while the food was still in their mouths, the Lord "put to death the sturdiest among them, cutting down the young men of

Israel" (v. 31). And still it made no difference. The people continued to sin and ignore God.

The Lord knows when our souls are grieved. Our Father in heaven is full to overflowing with compassion. But when we demand that He fix things now, that He resolve matters according to our agenda, it shows we've missed everything He's taught us. We need to allow room for His perfect will when we make our requests. "This is the confidence we have in approaching God," the apostle John writes: "that if we ask anything *according to his will,* he hears us. And if we know that he hears us—whatever we ask—we know that we have what we asked of him" (1 John 5:14–15).

We need to let God be God.

"The demanding and twisting we go through can often lead us down unhealthy roads," Bob Glaus says. "Those were incredibly difficult days after Wes was diagnosed. Did we question? Absolutely. But it wasn't, 'Why us?' or 'This isn't fair!' It was more, 'Father, what do we need to do to get Wes through this? What do we need to do to get *us* through this?' We weren't angry with God. We were fearful of the road that lay before us."

"For me, it came down to two choices," Jan Glaus says. "I can go through this with God, or I can go through this without God. And going through it without Him would mean darkness and death. As much as it hurts, it's better to go through a crisis with God. That's what leads to a future and an eternal hope."[2]

A God-Centered Future

I love the faithful attitude of Bob and Jan Glaus. I can't imagine what it would be like to discover that either of my two boys, Trent or Troy, had a life-threatening illness. It would be heartbreaking. It would rock my world. And yet, I hope and pray that I would be able to respond as Bob and Jan did—by asking for God's guidance and help to make it through and by trusting in Him for the future.

Isn't that what hope is all about? Trusting in a better and brighter future. Trusting that the days ahead will be filled with meaning, love, and joy. The Lord offers us that future each and every day—if only we can wipe the tears from our eyes long enough to see it.

We face so many challenges that can disrupt our view. Some of us, especially because of the recent economic upheaval, are struggling to find or keep jobs and make rent or mortgage payments. A few of us, on the other hand, are so prosperous that we've taken our eyes off the Lord and our future. We're enjoying the good life now at the expense of eternity.

Some of us face relationship challenges. Some of us have experienced a devastating loss, either a divorce or the death of a loved one. Some moms and dads are in anguish over rebellious or missing sons and daughters.

Some of us have filled our schedules to the max and are overwhelmed by busyness. Others are feeling trapped in dull jobs and routine lives. Some are ensnared by addictions such as alcohol, drug abuse, or pornography.

And then there are issues of faith. Either we drift through our lives, feeling spiritually empty and disconnected from God, or we feel so burdened by trouble and tragedy that doubt and despair take us prisoner.

The institutions of marriage and family are taking plenty of hits too. Our judges continue to rewrite the traditional and biblical definition of marriage. Divorce remains an unconscionably common first option for struggling husbands and wives. The number of single-parent homes continues to rise. Thousands of children are abandoned or orphaned each year and don't have even one parent to cling to. Hundreds of thousands more have no chance at any future when they are legally aborted in the first weeks or months of life.

The church also faces issues. Many believers are falling away from regular church attendance, in some cases replacing their Bible-based religion with a more personal brand of spirituality. To counter this alarming trend, some churches bend so far to be "relevant" and "seeker friendly" that they lose their biblical moorings. Other churches get lost in routine. They minister to their congregation, but only superficially, and have no influence in the outside world.

Don't get me wrong. Many, many people, families, and churches in the United States and around the world are thriving in faith and making a difference for the Lord's glory. They rest in His will and, as a result, discover their destiny.

For many of the rest, however, something is missing. It may be that we lack the confidence and strength derived from a God-centered vision of the future.

Signposts to Destiny

You've probably read or heard of a book by pastor Rick Warren titled *The Purpose Driven Life.* More than thirty million copies have been printed and sold or distributed around the world since its publication in 2002.

The subtitle for Rick's book is "What on Earth Am I Here For?" I think it speaks to the primary reasons why so many millions invest in Rick's words. People are searching for meaning and for assurance about their purpose. They want to know why they've been given this gift of life so they can step forward with confidence.

Many business owners I spoke with recently were shaken by our country's economic crisis. They candidly talk about the difficult predicament the tight economy put them in. Many remain concerned about having to cut staff in order to be financially viable. Others know they will lose their family business and, with it, their entire life savings if sales don't improve. Clearly, many business owners are worried about the future.

It's true that many of us have had it easy for a long time. We've enjoyed living in nice homes, driving nice cars, and wearing comfortable clothes. We've had a reasonably robust economy compared to much of rest of the world. Which is why it's tempting to believe that such blessings are our birthright, an entitlement for us to enjoy forever. I'll admit it's kind of nice to have it easy. But the easy life doesn't last forever. God designed it that way.

Without wanting to sound insensitive to those hardest hit by such difficult times, it strikes me that the Lord may have used the down economy to "shake the tree" so hard that there's not a limb left to hang on to. Put another way, when the going gets really tough, there's no place to land except on the one true foundation—our relationship with Christ.

He holds our future in His hands.

I've come to see the benefit in all the shaking. As we go to our knees in challenging circumstances, we come face to face with our Creator. The real business of life gets done in His presence. Just Him and me. One on one. Father and son. Talking. Listening. Connecting without distractions. That's not just a good thing; it's the best place to be. It allows Him to do His work in our hearts and point us in the direction He wants us to go. It allows us to develop a new confidence about the future.

If you're not already facing some of the challenges described here, you soon will be. That's just how life on earth works. The question, then, during difficult times is not, "What is the president doing to stimulate the economy?" or "Why is God picking on me?" Rather, we ought to ask, "What does God want me to learn from these tough times?" and "Why is God shaking our culture so hard that there's nothing left to fall back on except Him?"

We must see our troubles as an opportunity to get back on track with God's will and agenda. Our trials are the signposts to our destiny. That's true not only for us as individual believers. Remember my friends in China who've been praying for greater persecution of the American church? It's also time for some genuine soul-searching within our congregations.

I believe the following questions can help move us closer to acquiring God's strength, knowing His vision for our future, and discovering the assurance that allows us to move into our destiny:

- Why am I here?
- What does God want to do with my life?
- How can I best use my gifts and talents to advance His kingdom rather than my own?
- How far can I trust my Lord?

Let's take these questions to our heavenly Father in prayer. We might be surprised and excited by where He leads. When we know and trust in our purpose—the destiny planned for us by the Lord—we can move ahead with confidence and strength.

My Vision

I understand that a number of people today are pessimistic about the future. They point to our nation's general lack of values and morals. They see that many people seem to possess a lackluster faith and focus more on self than sacrifice. People worry about an emphasis on materialism and worldly success and a staggering economy. They grow discouraged by government rulers and rulings that seem to have little foundation in reason, and by a population that shows too little resistance to misguided politicians and policies.

They fear for our future.

I share this concern, but I don't share the pessimism.

I believe that the state of our world shows that we—as individuals, families, churches, and a nation—are approaching some major decisions. Many of us stand at the fork in the road that leads to a choice between beaten, bitter, or broken before the Lord. I think our Father in heaven is going to shake the tree of our lives until we can't help but choose His way.

I have my own vision of our future, and it springs from a link to the past. I think that when historians look back on our time, they may decide that the twenty-first century was a sister to the first century.

Think back to the decadence and paganism of first-century Rome. In the first century, a mighty empire, influential throughout the world, was gradually destroyed from within by crumbling values and self-centered hedonism.

Sound familiar?

The early Christians refused to honor pagan gods or acknowledge the emperor as "Lord." They also "practiced a morality that
condemned the common Roman practices of abortion, infanticide,
abandoning infants, suicide, homosexual acts, *patria potestas* [Roman
fathers were given the power of life and death over their wives, children, and slaves], and the degradation of women. Their [Christians']
moral posture was one of the many reasons why they were harassed,
hated, despised, and often imprisoned, tortured, or killed. The
Romans made them into an army of martyrs."[3]

These were men and women of incredible faith and strong
courage. Their bold actions and sacrifice inspired generations to
investigate and ultimately accept the claims of Christ. Their impact
reaches to this day.

Gerald Sittser, author of *Water from a Deep Well*, relates the
account of a woman from the second century who had converted
from paganism to Christianity:

> She wanted her husband to embrace the new
> faith with her and so gently tried to persuade
> him to become a Christian. But he persisted
> in unbelief and immoral behavior. So she filed
> for a divorce. Enraged, her husband brought
> charges against her in a Roman court, claiming
> that she had left him without his consent. He
> also mentioned that she was a Christian, which
> was probably the more serious charge. He then
> singled out her pastor too, holding Ptolemaeus

responsible for her conversion. So Ptolemaeus was also arrested. After being tortured for some time, Ptolemaeus was brought before a Roman judge, Urbicus, who asked him just one question, "Are you a Christian?" When he confessed that he was, Urbicus ordered his execution. Then another man, Lucius, also present in the courtroom, stood up and protested the judge's arbitrary and unfair judgment. "What is the charge? He has not been convicted of adultery, fornication, murder … or of any crime whatsoever; yet you have punished this man because he confesses the name of Christian?" Urbicus replied, "I think you too are one of them." Lucius responded, "Indeed I am." So he ordered Lucius's execution too. The account ends with one final—and very telling—observation. "Lucius then acknowledged his gratitude," it reads, "realizing that he would now be set free of such evil masters, and would depart for the Father and the king of heaven."[4]

What propelled these Christians to take a public stand for their faith and give their lives? I believe it was the unswerving love of the Lord and a strong vision of a God-designed future—one that stretched beyond present life and into eternity.

I say to those of us who are believers today that a time approaches when we must demonstrate this kind of *strong* faith. We must prepare to lay down our lives for Christ, either in service or in sacrifice.

And the bedrock of this newfound commitment will be our suffering and brokenness before Him.

For us as individuals, I see a renewed dedication to standing up for our beliefs and taking the gospel to the world. I believe we'll see an increased spirit of sharing and service, whether it's in programs that care for the poor, widows, and orphans or in simply reaching out to neighbors and coworkers. I also see the church taking on an increased role in providing for the needy and downtrodden, both within its membership and in the larger community, nation, and world. In my vision of the future, the spirit of God's love for His children guides all of these changes. They will take root because of His compassion *and* His strength.

As the institution of marriage falls under attack in our nation, I believe the church will respond by renewing its commitment to biblical marriage—a union between one man and one woman, blessed by God—and by helping to strengthen those marriage relationships. As a result, I see a decline in the divorce rate within the church and stronger, more successful families.

My vision for the future also includes parents who show a greater devotion to teaching their children about the significance of Jesus Christ in their lives and what it means to live a godly life.

I am not a pie-in-the-sky optimist. There is trouble ahead, and it's going to hurt. This kind of transformation doesn't take place unless we sacrifice and go much, much deeper in our faith and trust in the Lord.

But God is shaking the tree.

It's time to get ready.

A tumultuous and ultimately glorious future awaits.

Daddy, Will You Pray with Me?

When four-year-old Wesley Glaus was diagnosed with acute lym-phoblastic leukemia, the Glaus family was keenly aware of both realities—the pain of the present and the peace of resting in a future held by God.

Wes underwent intensive chemotherapy treatments. To prevent infection, he stayed in a germ-free environment at the hospital—a room sealed off by a plastic screen or "bubble." Bob and Jan had to wear special suits, gloves, and masks to interact with their son. Jan stayed with Wes during the day, then Bob took over after work and stayed until Wes fell asleep in the evening.

Before the diagnosis, Wes didn't really have time for Jesus. In Wes's mind, Jesus was the guy the Sunday school teacher talked about when Wes wanted to be outside running around on the playground. Jesus kept him from having fun. When Bob asked his son if he loved Jesus, Wes always answered, "Nope," and kept on running.

When Wes was in the bubble, however, his heart toward Jesus changed. In the evenings, before going to sleep, he began asking, "Daddy, will you pray with me tonight?"

For virtually the first time since he'd been born, Wesley's life had slowed down. He needed to hear the gentle whispers of God.

Bob and Jan prayed and waited. The treatments seemed to do their work. Then came the good news—Wesley's leukemia went into remission. Wes went home and enjoyed both Thanksgiving and Christmas with his family.

In January, however, the doctors were forced to deliver a differ-ent report. The "bad soldiers," as they all called Wesley's leukemia, were back.

Bob and Jan knew from previous conversations with the doctors that if the leukemia returned, chemotherapy would slow down the cancer, but it would no longer be enough to cure Wes. Their son's life was now completely in God's hands.

The afternoon after learning about the cancer's return, Bob and Wes took a walk near their home. "Wes, what do you think about those bad soldiers coming back?"

"Dad," Wesley said, "I don't want to talk about it." He needed time to process what was happening.

A few days later, Bob was in the bathroom with Wes, cleaning and drying him after a bath. They talked about the future.

"Someday Jesus will find you a wife," Bob said. "You'll get married, and she'll have your babies."

A strange look came over Wes's face. "Dad," he said, "I don't want to get old."

"You don't want to be old enough to ride a motorcycle?" Bob said.

Wes dropped his head. A single tear squeezed out of one eye and rolled down his cheek.

"Wes," Bob said in a quiet voice, "is it that you're afraid those bad soldiers won't let you get old?"

Wes nodded. "Yeah."

Bob asked Jan to join them, and together they talked about it. Wes admitted that he worried about dying and being away from his mom and dad.

"Wes," Jan said, "in heaven, one day is as a thousand years, and a thousand years is as a day. If you go to heaven soon, it'll be just like going to sleep, and when you wake up, we will be there. We'll be just down the hall."

Hope and Going Home

Bob and Jan continued to pray for healing for Wes, but they also accepted that healing might not be part of God's plan. Then, during a session with their church home group, a guest speaker told of receiving a word from the Lord for a family with a sick child. The word included a passage from Ezekiel: "And when I passed by you and saw you struggling in your own blood, I said to you in your blood, 'Live!' Yes, I said to you in your blood, 'Live!'" (Ezek. 16:6 NKJV).

"When that word came, it seemed like a message from God directly to us," Bob says. "From that point, we lived in hope that He would heal Wes. We believed it."

Despite the struggles and uncertainties, the Glaus family found ways to enjoy life and each other. They even took a skiing vacation at Lake Tahoe. Wes laughed as he skied. They looked forward to a miracle.

Bob, Jan, and Wesley chose to continue the chemo treatments for a time. Then the day came when a different, stronger medication would be required to prolong Wes's life. It would leave him with sores from his mouth to his stomach and mean staying full time in the hospital.

The Glauses decided to end the treatments. If God was going to heal Wesley, now was the time.

They took Wes home. He quickly and steadily declined. One morning, Bob knelt beside Wesley as he lay in his bed. "Wes, are you ready to be with Jesus?" Bob asked.

Wes looked up. "Yes," he said.

"Really?"

"Yes."

"Are you afraid?"

"No. Nuh-uh."

During nine months of treatments, the Lord had done amazing work in Wesley's heart. For most of the rest of that day, Wesley rested on the family room sofa. Eventually he couldn't see. Later, he drifted in and out of awareness.

That evening, as Bob sat beside his nearly comatose son, Bob's mother stood behind them.

"I guess we didn't get our miracle," she said in a voice choked with emotion.

"Mom, it's not over yet," Bob said. He still trusted the Lord for victory.

Soon after, Bob sat with Alese, then seven years old, and talked about what was happening. "If the Lord does take Wes home to heaven, it will be the best for him and the best for us," Bob said. "There may be a time in our home where we won't be as happy as in the past, but the Lord will heal us. He'll bring happiness and joy back."

Alese smiled and went to sleep.

That night, as Bob cradled his only son in his arms and tears flowed down his cheeks, Wesley Glaus went home.

In the morning, Bob walked into Alese's room and sat next to her on her bed. He told her that her brother was now with Jesus.

"Yeah. I kinda thought so," she said. "I could hear him breathing hard. I thought Jesus would take him."

Bob stroked his daughter's hair. "What do you think about that?"

"Well … I think he's the lucky one."

For Bob, peace with Wes's death did not come as quickly. He felt hurt and confused by God. He'd been ready to accept the Lord's will, whatever that might be. But then came the word and the message from Ezekiel. It had seemed like a promise. Had all their hope been for nothing?

At first, there was no response to Bob's questions. Yet as he grieved, meditated, and continued to converse with God, an unexpected answer began to write its way onto Bob's heart.

"After Wes relapsed, our house was never a gloomy place," Bob says. "There wasn't any dourness, any 'Oh, no, how could this be happening to us?' Our home was always filled with life. It could have been very different, but we had such hope.

"God allowed us and Wesley to live in the fullness and joy of life right up to the time when he went home to Jesus. Today, I am grateful for that."

Tears of Anticipation

It's been more than twenty years since Wesley Glaus joined Jesus in heaven. That difficult experience, along with continued Bible study, prayer, and conversation with the Lord, gave Bob and Jan a perspective that I find so encouraging. Their suffering, combined with the love and compassion of our heavenly Father, allowed them to focus on a God-centered future. And today, they have a vision of strength.

In so many ways, their vision is what this book is all about.

"Where your treasure is, there your heart is also," Jan says. "When your treasure is your child and he's with Jesus, your 'earth eyes' turn in a different direction. It makes you long and have a desire for eternity. When I think of being able to meet Jesus, I sure hope Wes is in His arms. It's going to be a tie on who I go to first!

"As a mother I am thankful God has given us two more wonderful treasures, our daughters Cecilee and Haven. God is so very good to us while we are here and then in the hereafter."

Bob speaks of the struggle of our earthly lives.

"If we think God's job is to make us happy and keep us trial free, we'll be sorely disappointed," he says. "Our life in Christ is a death sentence and an eternal life sentence at the same time. When we turn to Christ, our commitment is to be people of His kingdom, not of this world's kingdoms.

"For the first three years after Wes went home, I was praying every day, 'Lord, it would be easier if You just took me home than for me to live today. But here I am, and I'm going to do my best to keep doing what You are calling me to do.' Not a day goes by that I don't think of Wesley. I can be singing, and suddenly tears start pouring out of my eyes. But I've found that if I stay close to the Lord day by day, He uses that pain. He turns my tears of sorrow into tears of anticipation. These things we've longed for will become more real than what we see right now.

"There is a great, great day coming, and I can hardly wait."[5]

Epilogue

Throughout this book we explored the topic of strength. If you're like me, you've concluded that the most formidable and powerful strength—the kind that endures and hopes even when all seems hopeless—is found in only one source: the Lord of Lords and King of Kings. His is an eternal strength, unchangeable and unbreakable. It is available to you and me—not because we deserve it, but because He loves us.

One of the Bible's most eloquent descriptions of His strength and love is found in Psalm 62. I hope it will encourage you in troubled times as much as it encourages me.

> Find rest, O my soul, in God alone;
>   my hope comes from him.
> He alone is my rock and my salvation;
>   he is my fortress, I will not be shaken.
> My salvation and my honor depend on God;
>   he is my mighty rock, my refuge.
> Trust in him at all times, O people;

> pour out your hearts to him,
> for God is our refuge.
>
> Lowborn men are but a breath,
>   the highborn are but a lie;
>   if weighed on a balance, they are nothing;
>   together they are only a breath.
>
> Do not trust in extortion
>   or take pride in stolen goods;
>   though your riches increase,
>   do not set your heart on them.
>
> One thing God has spoken,
>   two things have I heard:
>   that you, O God, are strong,
> and that you, O Lord, are loving.
> (Ps. 62:5–12)

God's strength and love were evident to a couple named Mahlon and June Stoltzfus during a time when His character and divine attributes were most needed. In November 2008, Mahlon and June had just attended a Focus on the Family marriage conference in Bermuda when they received news that every parent dreads. Their son had been seriously injured in a car accident near their home in Gordonville, Pennsylvania. He had driven around a blind curve and crashed into a farmer's combine that blocked both sides of the road.

Mahlon and June arranged to return home on the earliest possible flight the next morning. Together they endured one of the longest nights of their lives. Questions circled endlessly in their minds. How badly was Brent injured? Would they be able to talk to their son again?

Even more important to this family of faith was Brent's standing with Jesus. He'd been raised in a Christian home and committed his life to Christ at a young age, but evidence of the Lord's presence often seemed absent. Brent was still trying to find his way in life. Was his salvation secure?

As Mahlon lay in bed that night, he recalled one of the messages he'd heard at the marriage conference, one that had made an impression on him at the time: Give thanks in all circumstances, for this is God's will for you.

Lord, Mahlon wondered, *what are we to give thanks for now?*

The next morning, as Mahlon and June waited at the airport to board their flight, a new phone call revealed that the situation was even worse than they'd feared. Brent, their only son, twenty years old and just a week away from achieving his dream of graduating from an auto mechanic's school, was brain dead.

The news, of course, devastated the couple. June's prayers narrowed to one urgent request: "Lord, please let him have had one minute to make peace with You."

At the Pennsylvania hospital later that day, Mahlon and June saw their son for the last time. Though his body was still present, the boy they'd raised and loved was clearly no longer with them. By the end of the next day, doctors disconnected the machines and tubes that kept Brent's body functioning, and he was pronounced dead.

One hospital staff member told June that Brent had died instantly. It triggered a fresh wave of grief for Mahlon and June—it meant he'd never had that minute with God. Then another staff member said that Brent was still breathing when he arrived at the hospital. It gave Mahlon and June a thread of hope. But which story was the truth?

At the urging of a friend, June prayed to the Lord, asking for a sign. They had to know.

Love for a Stranger

The sign came on a Saturday, the day after Brent's burial. Mahlon's brother Freiman had come from New York for the burial and memorial service. On Friday, he'd gone to a local barber for a haircut and mentioned his nephew's tragic accident. The barber's response shocked him.

"My daughter was following that combine at the time of the accident," he said. "She was with Brent."

On Saturday, Mahlon and June learned about the barber's daughter, whose name was Megan. Soon Megan told them her story.

A community college student, Megan owned a horse that boarded on a farm in the area. Though she normally didn't visit her horse on school days, she'd decided this particular day to go riding after her classes. On the way, she stopped at a pizza shop for a bite to eat. Then, while driving toward the farm, she spotted a dog lying on the side of the road. She turned around to check on it, but since the dog was dead and there was nothing she could do, she got back in her car and continued on.

Because of the timing of those events, Megan reached an inter-section just a quarter-mile from the farm at the moment that a large combine passed by. She turned left into the lane behind the combine. As they approached a curve, she heard a bang and saw smoke rising from the other side of the combine.

Something told Megan to jump out of her car. She ignored the combine driver, who was on his cell phone and nearly hysterical, and ran to the other side of the combine.

Megan heard a whimpering noise—it sounded like a baby. She peered under the combine and realized that a car had crashed and was pinned underneath. She crawled under the combine and saw a young man trapped in his seat, his body partially twisted out the driver's side door. He had a handsome face. Shards of glass were sprinkled in his brown hair. There was also a great deal of blood.

Megan quickly realized the young man was dying.

She said a prayer for both of them and took the man's hand. She asked him, "Can you hear me?" He tried to answer, but no words came.

He squeezed her hand instead.

Megan felt an amazing, overwhelming love welling up inside her for this stranger. She knew time was short. "If you have something to say to God," she told the young man, "say it now."

Bystanders began to arrive, but they kept their distance. They urged Megan to get away, saying the car might explode. Megan stayed, picking glass out of the young man's hair and continuing to hold his hand.

A few minutes later, the young man grew quiet. Still Megan stayed.

Finally, paramedics arrived and shooed Megan away. They wouldn't even tell her the young man's name. Only later, by searching on the Internet, did she discover who Brent was. When the invitation came to speak with Brent's parents, she was grateful for the opportunity.

Mahlon and June are grateful too—not for losing Brent, but for the way God arranged events so that a caring stranger could love and comfort their son in his final moments and guide him to a last opportunity to make peace with the Lord. As far as Mahlon and June are concerned, that string of "coincidences" led to a predestined, divine appointment.[1]

Through their grief, Mahlon and June have continued to give thanks in all circumstances—to look for blessings each and every day. This thankfulness protected them from anger and bitterness. Instead they saw God's goodness and continue to trust Him. It has been a way to choose the broken path.

In the midst of tragedy, God gave them strength.

The Beginning of Life

We live in an unyielding, often harsh world. Strength isn't a luxury. It's something we need in order to survive and thrive. We have seen in this book that strength can be ours and that it may be found in unexpected places. In God's kingdom, the weak are mighty, the helpless are powerful, and death is the beginning of life. I hope that encourages you as much as it does me.

The first step toward genuine, lasting strength is to invite Jesus to be the Lord of your life. If you have not made that commitment, I pray that you will take the opportunity to do so now. As Megan told

Brent, "If you have something to say to God, say it now." All it takes is a prayer from the heart—perhaps something like this:

> Lord Jesus, I need You. I can't make it on my own.
> I believe that You are the Son of God and that You
> died on the cross to free me from my sins. Please
> forgive all my sins and give me a new life in eternity
> with You. Amen.

Wherever you are in your faith and in the struggles of life, I urge you to call out daily to our heavenly Father. I can guarantee that He will hear your words. I can also say with complete confidence that He can turn your tears of sorrow into tears of anticipation.

No matter what you face today, the Lord understands what you're going through. He may not remove the pain, but He knows how to use it for His good purposes. He is standing by to walk through it with you.

He is always ready to offer you His strength and love.

Acknowledgments

There are always so many people who should be recognized after compiling a book. I've been blessed to have great and dear friends alongside me in this task. First, to Cris Doornbos, president of David C Cook—thank you for our friendship. Your encouragement has strengthened me in many ways. Also, to the great team at Cook, including Dan Rich, Ryan Dunham, and Don Pape for their dedication and desire to see Christ lifted up through the written word. To Alex Field, Brian Thomasson, Terry Behimer, Ingrid Beck, Caitlyn York, Amy Kiechlin, and Rule29 for helping bring this book to life.

To the Focus on the Family board for their confidence and inspiration. I see God in your lives in every phone call and in every meeting. To Dr. Dobson for his reminder to mend the brokenhearted. He has done that so well over the years. To the team at Focus on the Family for helping so many people find their way, which helps us to find our own. To the counselors who helped Jean think through the issue of depression, including C. Soozi Bolte, MACL, MC, LPC, LISAC. Thank you!

Also, thanks to Charlie and Patty Renfroe for their generosity. I was able to finish the last chapter at their beach house with Jean and the boys near my side. Thank you! To Jim Lund, my collaborator on this project. Your word craft is warm like your heart. It has been a great pleasure to work with you. To Greg Johnson, my agent and friend.

A special note of gratitude goes to the people who shared in interviews their personal and often heartwrenching stories for this book: Mahlon and June Stoltzfus, Bob and Jan Glaus, Diane Fassel, Todd Pierce, Drew Wills, Leslie McGill, and Amy Tracy.

Finally, to the many wonderful people who support Focus on the Family with their prayers and resources. You inspire me each and every day to represent the Lord with all my heart. Thank you for believing in the mission to help families thrive in Christ.

Notes

Chapter 1

1. David and Marie Works, *Gone in a Heartbeat* (Carol Stream, IL: Tyndale House, 2009).
2. Lori Mangrum, "I Was Panic-Stricken," *Today's Christian Woman,* http://www.christianitytoday.com/tcw/1997/sepoct/7w5050.html.
3. Works, *Gone in a Heartbeat.*
4. Mangrum, "I Was Panic-Stricken."

Chapter 2

1. Used with permission.
2. Alvin J. Schmidt, *How Christianity Changed the World* (Grand Rapids, MI: Zondervan, 2004), 19.
3. Schmidt, *How Christianity Changed the World,* 26.
4. Heather Sells, "China's Christians Face More Persecution," CBN News, August 1, 2008, http://www.cbn.com/CBNnews/419530.aspx.
5. NewsRoom, *Voice of the Martyrs,* http://www.persecution.com/public/newsroom.aspx (accessed February 19, 2010).

6. "North Korea Reportedly Kills Bible Distributor," *Bend Bulletin,* July 25, 2009.

7. Mary Frances Bowley, *A League of Dangerous Women* (Colorado Springs, CO: Multnomah, 2007), 26, 229.

8. Aleksandr I. Solzhenitsyn, *The Gulag Archipelago: 1918-1956. An Experiment in Literary Investigation,* vol. 2, trans. Thomas P. Whitney (New York: HarperCollins, 1973; Boulder, CO: Westview, 1998), 615–617.

9. John Piper, *Desiring God* (Sisters, OR: Multnomah, 2003), 265.

10. Joyce A. Coffin, "Zachary," *Chicken Soup for the Christian Family Soul* (Deerfield Beach, FL: Health Communications, 2000).

Chapter 3

1. James Lund and Peb Jackson, *A Dangerous Faith* (Colorado Springs, CO: WaterBrook, 2008), 171–179.

2. "National Statistics," American Foundation for Suicide Prevention, 2006, http://www.afsp.org/index.cfm?fuseaction=home. viewpage&page_id=050fea9f-b064-4092-b1135c3a70de1fda.

3. Tom Bowers, "Someone I Had to Forgive," *Guideposts,* January 1999, quoted in Lourdes Morales-Gudmundsson, *I Forgive You, But …* (Nampa, ID: Pacific Press, 2007), 136–137.

4. Leslie Haskin, *Between Heaven and Ground Zero* (Minneapolis, MN: Bethany House, 2008), 33–117.

5. Ibid., 133–134.

6. Ibid., 137–138.

7. Lund and Jackson, *A Dangerous Faith,* 186.

8. Bowers, "Someone I Had to Forgive," quoted in Morales-Gudmundsson, *I Forgive You, But …,* 136–137.

Chapter 4

1. Dr. James and Shirley Dobson, *Night Light for Parents* (Sisters, OR: Multnomah, 2002), 272.

2. Hiroo Onoda, *No Surrender* (Tokyo: Kodansha International, 1974), 14.

3. Bowley, *A League of Dangerous Women*, 222–223.

Chapter 5

1. Charlie and Lucy Wedemeyer, *Charlie's Victory* (Grand Rapids, MI: Zondervan, 1993), 180–181.

2. Ibid, 182.

3. Ibid., 285.

4. Ibid.

5. Larry Crabb, *Shattered Dreams* (Colorado Springs, CO: WaterBrook, 2001), 158–159.

6. Patrick Morley, *The Man in the Mirror* (Grand Rapids, MI: Zondervan, 1997), 116–117.

Chapter 6

1. Bill Watterson, *Scientific Progress Goes "Boink"* (Kansas City, MO: Andrews and McMeel, 1991), 118.

2. Used with permission.

3. Jennifer Rothschild, *Lessons I Learned in the Dark* (Sisters, OR: Multnomah, 2002), adapted in Dobson, *Night Light for Parents*, 244–45.

4. Dennis Kizziar, *Hope for the Troubled Heart* (Bend, OR: Maverick Publications, 2008), 47–48.

5. Randy Alcorn, *The Grace and Truth Paradox* (Sisters, OR: Multnomah, 2003), 84.

6. Used with permission.

Chapter 7

1. Phil Callaway, *Who Put the Skunk in the Trunk?* (Sisters, OR: Multnomah, 1999), 35–40.

2. Laurence Gonzales, *Deep Survival* (New York: W. W. Norton & Company, 2003), 41.

3. "Depression—Out of the Shadows: Statistics," Public Broadcasting Service, http://www.pbs.org/wgbh/takeonestep/depression/pdf/dep_stats.pdf.

4. Used with permission.

Chapter 8

1. Stormie Omartian, *The Power of a Praying Wife* (Eugene, OR: Harvest House, 1997), 16–17, and Stormie Omartian, *The Power of Praying Husband* (Eugene, OR: Harvest House, 2001), 18, 21–22.

2. Rob Parsons, *Bringing Home the Prodigals* (Colorado Springs, CO: Authentic, 2008), 6–7.

3. Used with permission.

Chapter 9

1. Julie Bryant, "A Story of Integrity … Unknown Student Thanked," *Omnibus Online,* September 19, 2002, http://media.www.omnibusonline.com/media/storage/paper193/news/2002/09/19/TheGallery/A.Story.Of.Integrity.Unknown.Student.Thanked-276472.shtml.

2. *Merriam-Webster's Collegiate Dictionary,* tenth edition, s.v. "Character."

3. Tim Kimmel, *Little House on the Freeway* (Portland, OR: Multnomah, 1987), 67–70.

4. Anne Beiler, *Twist of Faith* (Nashville, TN: Thomas Nelson, 2008).

5. Ibid., 224–225.

6. Lucille Lind Arnell, *Old-fashioned Virtues of Our Swedish "Mumma"* (Iowa City, IA: Penfield Books, 2002), 12–14.

7. Used with permission.

8. Rebecca Manley Pippert, *A Heart Like His* (Wheaton, IL: Crossway, 1996), quoted in Alice Gray, compiler, *Stories for a Faithful Heart* (Sisters, OR: Multnomah, 2000), 108-109.

Chapter 10

1. Used with permission.

2. John Piper, *The Pleasures of God* (Sisters, OR: Multnomah, 2000), 198–199.

Chapter 11

1. Used with permission.

2. Ibid.

3. Schmidt, *How Christianity Changed the World,* 27.

4. Herbert Musurillo, ed., The Acts of the Christian Martyrs (New York: Oxford University Press, 1972), 63–85, quoted in Gerald L. Sittser, Water from a Deep Well (Downers Grove, IL: InterVarsity, 2007), 40.

5. Used with permission.

Epilogue

1. Used with permission.

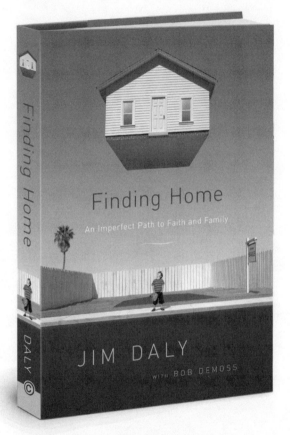